God Can Change You

They Said I Wouldn't Make It

Pastor Tommy Campbell, Jr.

Copyright © 2008 by Pastor Tommy Campbell, Jr.

God Can Change You
They Said I Wouldn't Make It
by Pastor Tommy Campbell, Jr.

Printed in the United States of America

ISBN 978-1-60477-902-8

All rights reserved solely by the author. The author guarantees all contents are original and do not infringe upon the legal rights of any other person or work. No part of this book may be reproduced in any form without the permission of the author. The views expressed in this book are not necessarily those of the publisher.

Unless otherwise indicated, Bible quotations are taken from The Hebrew-Greek Key Word Study Bible – King James Version of the Bible. Copyright © 1991 by AMG International, Inc.

www.xulonpress.com

To: My Bishop, My mentor, my spiritual father. Thank you for accepting me back into the family. Please forgive me for not dedicating this to you, but I dedicate this to you. Love always,

DEDICATION

I dedicate this book first to Jesus Christ. He is the one who delivered me, set me free and saved me. Next, I dedicate it to my wife, who has stuck by my side through thick and thin; to Bishop Vander D. Purcell, who has mentored me, been like a father to me, loved me and poured into me spiritually; to my mom and deceased grandparents; to my mother-in-law Valerie Scheier; to my best friend Erick Pryor; to Robert Beasley and Regina Ferguson who have blessed me; to Teresa and Akin Amusan; to Willie Murray, Kedric Simms, Melvin Langston, Noel Turnbull, Pastor Roy Rogers, and Pastor Kevin A. Williams; and to so many others. All these people I love so very much who have made a major impact in my life.

CONTENTS

Introduction	My Life	ix
One	Spiritual Insight	37
Two	If I Can Just Get Through the Roof	75
Three	You're Suffering Won't Last Forever	83
Four	Stretch Out Your Hand	97
Five	It's Time for You to Clean Your House	111
Six	God Wants to Give You Peace During Your Storm	121
Seven	You Can Attack Me But You Can't Destroy Me	133
Eight	Whatever Is In You Will Come Out of You	145
Nine	The Chains in Your Life are Loose	163
Ten	God is Calling Your Name	173
Eleven	A Renewed Mind	191

Twelve	Stop Criticizing	199
Thirteen	Nail Yourself to the Cross	207
Fourteen	If You Only Knew the Gift	215
Fifteen	I Have to Get to my Destiny	223
Sixteen	Don't Make the Kingdom of God a Secret	227
Seventeen	It's Time to Come Out of the Tomb	243
Eighteen	Your Haters are Setting You Up	257
Nineteen	Take the Limits Off of Me and Release Me	269
Twenty	You've Come Too Far to Turn Back Now	283
Twenty-One	You're Too Gifted to be Defeated	297
Twenty-Two	You Ain't Finished Yet	309
Twenty-Three	Don't Look Back Now	323
Twenty-Four	When the Going Gets Tough	335
Twenty-Five	Receiving Wisdom	343
	Final Word	349

INTRODUCTION

MY LIFE

My name is Tommy Campbell Jr., and I was born in Lumberton, N.C. on August 7, 1978. I was raised by my maternal grandparents, who are now deceased. I went through a lot of difficulties in my life. In this chapter, I want to focus primarily on my life, what I went through, and the things that have taken place in my life, to show the young people and adults of this generation that Jesus Christ can save you at a young age. No matter what you have done or what kind of lifestyle you are in, Jesus Christ can deliver you and set you free from the yoke and bondage of sin. The Lord told me years ago that I would be a writer and an author. It was spoken and prophesied over my life that I would write books. God led me to write this first book about my life and what I have been through. I was told by many people that I would never amount to anything, and so many people turned their back on me. I would often wonder why I was always getting hurt by people. I wondered why when I did something wrong, I was always the one who got caught. The things I been through in my life should have killed me. When I look back on my life, I often wonder how in the world I made it through all of that. That is why there is no devil in hell that can tell me that God isn't real. Jesus Christ is alive and God did raise His Son Jesus from the dead. The Bible says in John 3:16, "For God so loved the world, that he gave his only begotten Son, that whosoever believeth in him should not perish, but have everlasting life." I like to go further into the verse where it says, "For God sent not his Son into the world to condemn the world; but that the world through him might be saved." (John 3:17) In other words, God did send his Son Jesus into the world to save us and to redeem us or to buy us back, and to bring us out of the yoke of bondage. God also didn't send his Son Jesus to condemn us or to make us feel guilty of our sins, but to save us or to save the world through Jesus. As I was growing up, I experienced a lot of challenges in life. I want to talk about my life and talk about who God is to me and who God can be to the readers of this book.

When I was first born, the devil tried to kill me and I didn't understand why I was always sick. I almost died several times when I was little. The devil tried to take me out with asthma and bronchitis. I would have to get breathing treatments all the time when I was little. When I look back on my life now, then I realize that satan knew that God was going to use me in the Ministry, and use me mightily in this earth. So satan was trying to take me out early.

One thing I will say for the readers of this book is that when God has a anointing on your life for Ministry, you can look to be attacked by satan. He is really fearful of you, and the reason being is because he knows how effective you are going to be for God, if you ever get converted. So satan is trying to keep you entangled with the yoke of bondage so you can never fulfill your destiny and your purpose on this earth.

That is what satan was doing with me. He was trying to destroy me before I realized who I am in Christ. One of the things I have realized is that satan doesn't even mind if you proclaim you are Christian. Anybody these days, if you ask them if they are a Christian, they will say, "I am a Christian." But when you start talking about living holy, and setting yourself apart from the world, and letting go of the world to live for Christ, it is then that the enemy will begin to get intimidated. Satan knows if you ever start truly seeking to live a holy life, and seek to set yourself apart from the world, and to find out who you are as a Christian, he then knows you will be a threat to his kingdom.

Satan tried so hard to destroy me as I was growing up. As far as I can remember, I was kind of back and forth with my parents and my grandparents. For the most part, I stayed with my grandparents on my mother's side for years. My parents were doing their own thing. The only positive role models I had were my grandparents. They did the best they could, as far as trying to raise me. They raised me up in a Presbyterian Church called Bethany Presbyterian, and the Pastor was named Reverend Walker. My grandmother was kind of disabled and had arthritis, and I remember him coming over and serving her Holy Communion. I would gaze into her eyes to see the excitement when he would come and see her and serve her Holy Communion. I would go to Sunday School at this Presbyterian Church, would go to Easter Egg Hunts and was in the Children's Choir, but there was still something missing. I often wondered how in the world I ended up making the decisions I made when I had the kind of grandparents I had. As I grew older, I started wondering where my parents were, and I yearned for them, and wanted to be with them. As I got older, my grandmother didn't try to make like she was my mother, even though she carried that role, but she didn't lie to me. I remember when I would have Christmas at my grandmother's, I would wonder what Santa was going to bring me, and I got lots of toys that were from my parents that had brought them over to my grandmother's. I never understood why I had to be with my grandmother, but as I got older I realized it. My mother got married at a very young age, and they were not Christians. It was me, my baby brother, and my older sister. I remember when I was a child how I would be so sick with bronchitis and asthma and had to go to the hospital to get breathing treatments. I came so close to death, but the hand of God would bring me out every time. I never understood why God did, but now I understand. The whole time, God was setting me up to be used in the Ministry and I didn't even know it.

One thing I have realized is that when there is a call on your life for Ministry, you are a threat to satan's kingdom. When God has a plan for your life, you can look to be attacked by satan. In Matthew 4:1-11 Jesus is tempted by satan in the desert. The Bible says, "Then was Jesus led up of the Spirit into the wilderness to be tempted of the devil." (Matt 4:1) God showed me that before promotion comes, you first have to be tested. God is infinite; meaning there is no limit to His ability, and God is not subject to time and space. God is not bound by earthly specifications and God can do anything whenever he wants to. God is Spirit, and God tests us not so God can know what is in us, but so we may know what is in us. God is omniscient; meaning he is all knowing, God knows any and everything, and God lead Jesus in the desert so he could prepare Jesus for Ministry. You have a divine God who is now incarnate (meaning having a body) wrapped up in human flesh. Jesus is God, but was human as well. He was in flesh and he was subject to time and space and he couldn't be everywhere at the same time in his earthly body. So Jesus goes into the desert to be tempted by satan. What I realize is that God allowed me to go through what I went through only to make me stronger. The Bible says in Matthew 4:2, "And when he had fasted forty days and forty nights, he was afterward hungry." So that means Jesus was at His weakest point in life; he was hungry, weak and needed food. What you have to realize is that when you are spiritually vulnerable and weak in your flesh, then that is the time to draw close to Jesus. The Bible says in James 4:7-8, "Submit yourselves therefore to God. Resist the devil, and he will flee from you. Draw nigh to God, and he will draw nigh to you." There are three things you must do when you are weak in your flesh, because when you are weak in your flesh you will sin. My former professor once said, "Sin will take you further than you want to go." I must admit, sin did take me further than I wanted to go. Later on in this book, you will see how far it took me. I am also led to throw spiritual truths in this book as well, based off of scripture, so you will feel my heartbeat for God, see where my heart is and to help the readers who will come in contact with this book. My goal in this book is for you to see where I once was, where

God has brought me to now and to help you grow closer to God. In James 4:7-8, you must do three things and they are:

1. **Submit**: Meaning come under the authority of a higher power than yourself. For example, when you have a job, and you have your boss, you are submitting or doing whatever your boss tells you to do, simply because you know they are in charge. That is how it is with God; you submit to God simply because he is in charge; he is in charge of your soul. You submit to God simply because you know he is the creator, and that he is in control of everything.

2. **Resist the devil**: The word resist means to fight against or to oppose. That is what you are supposed to do is fight against the devil. One major way to fight against the devil is to submit to God. Resist the devil, and he will flee. So when you fight the devil with the Word of God then the devil has to leave you alone. But one thing you must understand is that satan is going to attack you until the day you die. The attack of satan stops when your time on this earth is up. As long as you are a sincere and true believer, then you will always be under attack from the enemy.

3. **Draw near to God**: If you draw near to God while you are weak in your flesh, then God will draw near to you. It is so simple. The devil has so many people tricked because he wants them to think it is so hard to live for God. I must say, it is challenging because you have an opposing force which is satan, but you have the power of the Holy Ghost. With the power of the Holy Ghost, it makes you armed and dangerous. Satan is a hater because he knows he will never have access to the Holy Ghost like we do.

So the three things to do when you are weak and you feel like you are about to sin are: submit to God, resist the devil and he will flee, and then draw near to God and God will draw near to you. One thing I have realized is that God will not force himself on anyone. God will only deal with those who have a heart for him. The Bible says in Matthew 4:3, "And when the tempter came to him, he said, If thou be the Son of God, command that these stones be made bread." Now that was a mistake right there, because satan is the tempter, and he knows that Jesus is the Son of the Living God. Being that he is so much of a deceiver, he still asks Jesus to turn these stones to bread. What you have to realize as a believer is that no matter how anointed you are or what kind of title you have, you can be a

Bishop, Apostle, Pastor, Elder, Evangelist, Prophet etc., you are not beyond being tempted. If you aren't careful, when you are weak, the tempter, which is satan, can cause you to spiritually turn your stones to bread.

I must say when I was growing up, I was always sick, and the devil secretly tried to kill me with my sickness. My grandmother taught me my ABC's, and my counting, and she taught me multiplication, and she taught me how to read. When I got in school as a kid, I had problems in school and I was considered slow. I flunked the first grade and got held back. I remember when the end of the school year came and it was time to go to the second grade, and I saw all of the kids going to the second grade, but I remember my 1st grade teacher saying, "Tommy stay in this class room." I said, "Why? Didn't I pass my grade to?" And she said, "No Tommy, you failed your grade." At that time I thought my life was over then, and I felt so embarrassed about flunking the first grade. I knew I tried, and I realize now that God will use your setbacks in life to get you to your destiny. God showed me that you will never know how to obtain true success until you have had an appointment with failure. God will really use the setbacks in life to promote you. In Genesis, Joseph was thrown in a pit and sold into Egypt by his brothers, who were envious and jealous of him. It seemed like his destiny was denied. It may have been delayed, but not denied. That is how it was for me when I was little and growing up. I always got into things, and it seemed like the devil was getting the best of me.

By the time I got to middle school, I started hanging out with the wrong crowd of kids. I was the type of kid that wasn't a leader, but I was a follower, and I always tried to fit in with the crowd. I wanted that acceptance from the kids, and I always did stupid stuff to get the other kids' attention and to make them laugh. I was the class clown, not realizing I was making a fool of myself. I thought it was significant what I was doing, when really it was definitely insignificant.

Once I got into middle school, then that was when I started staying with my parents. That wasn't the best thing, because all my parents would do was argue, and I grew up seeing that. When I was in middle school, I got caught cheating in school because I didn't believe in myself and I didn't think I was smart enough to pass on my own. My dad didn't spend time with me as I was growing up because he always worked. He never gave me the love I needed from him. At that time, my parents were not Christians at all. My parents didn't start proclaiming Christianity until I got older and they were much older. When I was in middle school, I would skip school, I was hanging around the wrong crowd of kids, and I was doing terrible in school. Then I wanted to start dating in middle school, and I had no one to tell me that I was too young to date and have a girlfriend. I was interested in a girl named Debbie, and we dated for a while, and then she got tired of me and wanted to date someone else. I was hurt by that so I built up a wall, and had low self esteem. Debbie was a very beautiful black girl then. I remember when I was in middle school my last day of school in middle school I left school with some of my friends, and the principal caught us, and came running after us, and we got away. So you see the devil was working on me and through me big time then, and I didn't even realize it. As I look back now, I thought what I was doing was right simply because I was trying to fit in. I never had my father to show me love like a real father, and I never understood why we could never have a father and son relationship. I would see how my mother was hurt and unhappy, and for a while it made me hate him. The way he treated me just added fuel to the fire, but today I can say I have forgiven him. Once I got in middle school and moved in with my parents I stopped going to church. I would go to church every now and then. When I started the 8th grade at Lumberton Junior High School, I really thought I was grown. I started playing and trying out for sports. I fell in love with the game of basketball. I wasn't that good then, and when tryouts came, all of my friends made the basketball team, and I got cut. I never understood why I would get cut when I was pretty good for my age. Then I started getting in trouble in Junior High School and got put in In-School-Suspension. So as I was growing up, the devil really had me under attack, simply because he knew I would be where I am today. As I was in Junior High School, I got interested in a Caucasian girl. We dated for a very short period of time and then she got interested in someone else. I just knew I was in love with her, and I felt like my whole world was over. Now mind you I was only in the 8th grade. God actually used my sister to save my life. If not, then there is no telling what would have happened, and I probably would be dead. My parents never even knew this at all, but my sister knew, and God used her to save my life.

It took me so long to get over this girl. By the time I got to High School, I was still hanging around the same kids I went to Middle School and Junior High School with. I happened to get involved in sports like basketball and track. I made the J.V. basketball team and I fell in love with the game of basketball. At that time, God kept me out of a lot of trouble by getting me involved in sports during high school. Once I got in high school, I started chasing women and my grades were suffering because I already had no confidence in myself. I wasn't honest in high school and me and my friends would cheat in school to get by. I started to have sex out of marriage when I was in the 11th grade. I started getting involved with the wrong females.

There was one Caucasian female in high school I got interested in, and I fell for her. She kind of led me on, and her name was Latisha. I got so interested in her until I went and stole a pair of jeans for her from J.C. Penney's. My friends would steal with me. I got caught and had to go to court when I was 16 years old. They didn't get caught, but I did and I took the blame for everything. The judge just made me do community service and didn't even put it on my record; that was the hand of God on that. My mom was really hurt, and she didn't understand why I took the blame for everything.

It got in the news paper what I had done, and I got kicked off of the basketball team. So I transferred to a school in Rowland, N.C. called South Robeson High School, and it was bad there too. I was a nice clean cut guy, and it was a small school. All of the girls were attracted to me because I was the new student. I happened to get interested in another Indian female and she led me on, and I then fell in love with her (what I thought was love). She hurt me and went for someone else. I never quite understood why I was always getting hurt. I couldn't see then what I see now, but God was using all of those things that happened in my past to get me to where I am now. The Bible says in Romans 8:28, "And we know that all things work together for good to them that love God, to them who are the called according to his purpose." So the enemy knew I had purpose in Christ Jesus and knew I had a Ministry in my spirit, and he was then trying to do everything he could to keep me from fulfilling and walking into my destiny and purpose. At this new High School, I noticed that a lot of the guys were jealous of me simply because I was new and clean cut, and all the females were showing interest in me, and I was talked about among them all. The ones that showed me friendship talked about me and back-stabbed me when my back was turned. There were times when I started to go back to church when I was in High School. I would go to church with my friend's aunt and uncle and I would hear the Gospel being preached, but I had a deaf ear to what the preacher was saying. I even went up for prayer before, but it didn't seem to do any good. The seed was planted, but boy did I still stray from God as I got older. Some way I went with my second cousin to a Jehovah Witnesses church called Kingdom Hall. I didn't know what I was opening myself up to, but the devil knew. Now I opened myself up to a religious spirit. I went there once or twice, and I didn't become a Jehovah Witness, I was just trying to be accepted by my friends and following the crowd rather than being a leader. I didn't know enough about Jesus to know that their religion was a false religion. Then the devil was even more deceivable; he sent some Mormons along in our neighborhood. They seemed so nice and I started hanging out with them and playing basketball with them. They offered to teach me about their doctrine and they came into my home and taught me. I don't remember what they taught me to this day, and that is a blessing. I would hang out with them, and I started going to their services on Sunday, and I got all of that false doctrine in my spirit. The next thing you know, they had me baptizing people. I was a filthy dirty sinner, and they had me baptizing. At that time, I didn't know it was a cult. I was 17 years old in the 11th grade.

So finally the Mormons that I hung out with, they were from Utah and moved back. Once they went back, I stopped going there, and that was a blessing. I simply went to their church because of how nice they were. They showed me what I thought was love, when it wasn't. Then around my senior year in High School, I noticed my mom taking interest in the Lord. She started talking a new talk, and she wanted to live for the Lord. I noticed she would get preaching videos by Bishop T.D. Jakes. I was trying to play college basketball, but my coach didn't think I was good enough to play college basketball. My grades were not good and I didn't do well on the SAT. I applied to Campbell University and didn't get in because of my grades and SAT score. I also applied to N.C. A&T State University and I didn't get accepted there either, so I applied to Shaw University in Raleigh, North Carolina, and got accepted.

One day before I went off to college, I was at home about to go play basketball. My mom had a Christian woman in our house and as I walked down the hall, she turned around and looked at me. She said, "Is that your son Melody?" My mom said yes, and she looked at my mom and said I was going to be a preacher. I thought to myself that this woman was crazy and had literally lost her mind. I got in my vehicle, and said to myself that she was crazy. I said to myself I am not going to be a preacher, I am going to play basketball at college, and go overseas and play professional basketball. I had the hoop dreams real bad. I thought that was what God wanted me to do was play college basketball, and to play overseas. I remember right before I went off to college for the first time, I was talking with my mom and she started crying. She said, "Son, I don't know what it is, but there is something special about you." So I went off to college at Shaw University in Raleigh, North Carolina. My freshmen year I tried so hard to play for the basketball team and I tried out and didn't make it. I was so hurt and I got involved with the wrong crowd, but somehow I managed to start going to church.

In 1998, I went to a church called the Upper Room Church of God in Christ in Raleigh, N.C. where the Senior Pastor's name is Pastor Wooden. I was sitting in the very back of the church and he was preaching exactly to me. He was stepping all on my toes. They were at their old facility at this time. I was so convicted of my sins and when he made that altar call I went up to the altar wanting to change. I was wearing all black and I was skinny and little. There were over 50 people at the altar and I was in the very back, stuck in the packed crowd. Somehow, he called me out and said, "Young man, come here." I was wondering why everyone started looking at me, and he said, "You sir, in the all black." He told me to come up in the pulpit where he was. I went and he anointed me and laid hands on me. He prophesied and said that God had some great things in store for me and that God was going to use me mightily. Now the devil witnessed that occasion, and immediately he started working on me. I got so caught up in wanting to play college basketball until I transferred from Shaw University to UNC Pembroke, going based off of no promise that I would play for this college. I got there and I tried out and the coach led me on thinking I was going to play, but he didn't let me. I was hurt and then I started drinking real bad, partying, and getting involved with the wrong crowd. Once I didn't make it at UNC Pembroke, I transferred to North Carolina A&T State University. I went home when school was over, before I went to NC A&T State University. It seemed like my mom was different; that she had really started seeking God. I could see that God was dealing with her. She had a lot of Bishop T.D. Jakes material and

I watched his videos when I was there because I had no church at home at that time. I must say, as I was watching Bishop T.D. Jakes preach, I knew he was a true Man of God. He was preaching with the power of God, and I got so convicted of my sins. I told my mom that I was going to live for God now. The devil knew I was getting closer to surrendering my all to God, so he was already setting me up for traps when I went to this new college I transferred to.

I went off to North Carolina A&T State University from UNC Pembroke. I was living for God for a while and I said I wasn't going to have sex again until I got married, but I was still full of lust and the enemy knew my weakness. So I was focused on trying to play college basketball for them, but the coach said that I wasn't able to try out and I had to wait a year. Then I got distracted again and started back drinking.

I met an African-American woman and I fornicated with her. I told her I was supposed to wait until I was married and that I was just coming to Christ. Right after we fornicated, I knew I was wrong and I popped in a Bishop T.D. Jakes video that my mom had given me. Then I had told her that I didn't want her and that I was a Christian now and that it would be better if she went her way and I went my way. Then the devil knew I was weak, and she wrote me a letter saying she wanted to be in a relationship with me and that she didn't want to lose me and that she was sorry, and that I was a good man, and that was what she needed was a man like me. Being that I was weak, I fell for it and I believed it, and we started dating. The next thing you know, I stopped going to church and I was listening to worldly music. We continued in our fornication and we dated for almost a year. I finally got tired of fornicating and I told her that we have to stop this or I am walking away. She said okay we will stop, not knowing that she was sent by the devil. The devil was really using her to keep me off track. She may have not known the devil was using her, but he used her big time. So then I fell in love with her and wanted to marry her. We started going to church together at Mount Zion Baptist Church where the Senior Pastor is Bishop George W. Brooks. That lasted a little while, and then she started wanting to have sex again so I fell back into it. When the end of the school year came, she started acting funny towards me. That is when I started to go through spiritually, and all of a sudden God started dealing with me. All of a sudden, I wanted to really live for God. I told her I would no longer continue in fornication with her and I wanted to marry her. All of a sudden, I started sensing evil and I started to realize I was called to the ministry and that I wanted to be in church all the time.

I happened to be sitting in class about to take a Spanish exam, and I started sensing evil and the atmosphere seemed uncomfortable and real weird. I started sensing evil, so I rushed through my exam and got out of there. When I was walking through the halls, it was like I could see evil and the atmosphere was so evil. I could sense and see demons on the people. It seems crazy, and it is taking a lot of faith for me to write this portion of this book. This was the year of 2000. I could not eat anything and I got so skinny. My ex had me thinking she was going to stick with me, and the whole time she was plotting to leave me once the school year ended in the spring. I got so sick in my body and I went to the doctor on campus. They ran every kind of test on me and could find nothing wrong with me. Then I went to other doctors in Greensboro, North Carolina, and they ran all kinds of test and could find nothing. I never understood why they couldn't find anything when I was feeling like I was.

My ex and I went to see my friend, who was an older strong Christian woman. I was in there crying so hard and saying I want God so bad and she prayed for me. Then my ex went home for the summer. I had created a yahoo email account for her, so I knew her password. We would email each other and something said go into here account I made for her. I went in it, and I saw where she was putting me down saying I was a Jesus freak, and that I was broke and had no money, and that my credit was messed up. She was telling her ex about what they used to do and that she wanted to meet him again. I was so hurt, so I called her and told her what I read. She asked me to forgive her and to take her back. Me being so weak, I took her back. Then finally she broke up with me, and boy was I tore up. I was depressed and I couldn't eat. My mom really watched me go through, and my mom watched me suffer for a long time. I went back to North Carolina A&T State University in 2001, and again I started sensing something evil. Now, all of a sudden, I was walking in the public loudly calling on Jesus and spitting up. I suppose it was God purging me, but at the time I didn't understand it. I was so scared and I assume it scared the other students, because they didn't understand what God was doing with me.

I started going back to Mount Zion Baptist Church under the leadership of Bishop George W. Brooks. I happened to be in a service where the college students were and this was after my break-up. All of a sudden, I started praising God and rose up crying real hard and crying out for the help of the Lord and they had to escort me out. Then this thing started happening again, and then it just got worse. I ran down the street calling on the name of Jesus and it seemed like I was being purged. I was spitting up and passed out. Someone called the ambulance because I was downtown passed out under the bridge. The next thing you know, I was in an ambulance calling on Jesus. I went into the hospital and was calling on Jesus, and they had me tied down to the bed. They sent me to a mental institution, simply because they didn't understand that it was spiritual. I stayed there for months and almost a year for the first time. I had met another female who said she would be there while I was going through. She gave up on me and married someone else that I knew. That caused me to build up a wall towards females, and I stopped trusting females simply because they would always lie to me and hurt me. They would say they would stay by my side during the very difficult times, but when I was under serious attack by satan, and going through purging and deliverance, they all turned their backs on me. All of my friends who were with me when I was in sin turned their back on me as well. The doctors said I would be messed up for the rest of my life, but God. I was in and out of the mental hospital for months. There were times when I went through and I was calling on Jesus because of what I was seeing and experiencing. I wasn't hurting anyone, but the public simply thought I was crazy and they didn't understand the spiritual side of it. The cops cuffed me for no reason and took me to the hospital. The cops asked me why I kept calling on Jesus. They asked what it was about Jesus that was making me call on His name like that. I was being purged, and I never knew I would publicly go through that. It was so terrifying and embarrassing, but I couldn't help it, because it was so terrifying. I recommend no one to go through what I went through. To this day, I still don't understand why I had to get it like that, but His thoughts are not our thoughts and His ways are not our ways.

We don't fully understand why God chooses to move like he moves, we just have to trust in him, and have faith that he will work it out. The cops were mistreating me and dragging me, and being violent. I was shocked when the cops were treating me like that, because I had harmed no one and had done nothing except what I went through. The only person that was there for me in the end of this and who watched over me was God and my friend Reverend Erick Pryor. Erick knew me when I was deep in sin and before I accepted the call to preach. He mentored me for years when I was at NC A&T State University. He prayed for me many nights in the dorm. It is a blessing to have someone that will believe in you and that will stick by you when no one else will. God always has a ram in the bush. God always has someone that will stick by your side no matter what. After I went through all of this, it changed my life forever. I started seeking God for real and I can say it did humble me, and I was a changed man. God showed me through his word and through prophetic voices that I was called to preach. When I was going through all of that, I couldn't see that, but God was cleansing me, purging me and getting me ready for Ministry. I still don't fully understand everything I went through, and I may never fully understand it all, but God doesn't have to explain anything to his people. Finally I stopped fornicating, and I waited for my wife. I studied God's Word a lot and I just began to seek the face of God. I always say that there is a price to pay for the anointing of God. In this transition, I experienced a lot of hurt in the church. The enemy knew he no longer had a hold on me, so once I got committed to the church he then started attacking me in the church. I served in churches by cleaning the churches, ushering, and teaching Bible study, and still experienced hurt in the church. I was even hurt by Pastors in the church, but I thank God I was mature enough to stay with God. I started to preach the Gospel around 2002. God had raised me up quickly in the last couple of years. I started as an Evangelist traveling and preaching the Gospel. I preached in National Conferences, Revivals, etc. I have been preaching now for about five years. Now I have gone 'From Falling to the Calling'.

As you can see, it was never in my plans to be a preacher. As I was growing up, I never intended to be a preacher. I was surrounded by so many fake ones who played church and faked the front. I always told myself that once I got saved, I was going to be for real.

Once you are saved, Holy Ghost filled and in Ministry, it seems like the enemy uses your family to attack you. Just like Jesus, when he went back to his home town, he could not do many miracles there. The Bible says he laid hands on a few, but many saw Jesus as what he used to be, a carpenter. They went by the fact that Mary was his mother and so they were looking from a fleshly perspective and they missed out on what God had from them. What I realize is that if God can take a messed up young man like me and change me, then God can change anybody. I was on my way to a burning hell, but God reached down and saved me and brought me out. What I realize is that sometimes the people, family, and friends who are most familiar with you are a little shocked when God begins to raise you up and use you in a mighty way.

God has brought me 'From Falling to the Calling'. Now, I am a Senior Pastor and traveling as an Evangelist, operating within the fivefold ministry. I give God the glory for it, according to Ephesians 4:11-12, "And he gave some, apostles; and some, prophets; and some, evangelists; and some, pastors and teachers; For the perfecting of the saints, for the work of the ministry, for the edifying of the body of Christ." I operate as a Pastor and an Evangelist at the age of 29. I used to be a sinner, and I was in the pit of sin, and in the valley, but God reached down in the valley, and saved me, delivered me, set me free, and filled me with the Holy Ghost. God has blessed me with a wonderful wife by the name of Dawn Marie Campbell and she has been a true blessing to me and to my Ministry. We met at church and I happened to go up to her. When I first laid eyes on her, I said to myself that she was the prettiest woman I have ever laid eyes on, and I knew there was something different about her. I started hanging out with her, and I noticed she was different because she was so quiet, and she never tried to come on to me at all. I told myself and her that I was waiting until I get married, and she agreed to that. So I really knew she was different. She started to travel with me when I would preach and she carried herself as a woman of God. She respected me for the preacher and man of God that I am, and we dated and we never fornicated. I sought God, and on March 06, 2005, after I had preached that Sunday out of town, I put on some Bishop T.D. Jakes Sacred Love Song CD, and I got down on my knees, and told her what kind of woman she was, and how she passed all of the tests with me, and how much I love her, and I asked her to marry me, and she said yes. Praise God!!!!!!! She said yes!!!!!!!!!!!!! Now we are still married going on two years, and I still love her to this day. She will tell you she never knew she was marrying a preacher, and I will tell you I never knew I was going to be a preacher, and I definitely didn't know I was going to Pastor. If you would have told me years ago that I was going to Pastor, then I would have thought you were crazy. My wife is very supportive and she is so humble and quiet.

That is my whole life in a nut shell, and you have seen what God can do and what he is still doing in me and through me. God has taken a young man that people didn't believe in, that people hurt, talked about, abused, mistreated, back-stabbed, lied on, and God has taken me and flipped the script on the enemy. Now God is using me mightily in the kingdom of God. The kind of people God wants are the ones that are difficult to change; God wants the ones who have done the most dirt, because God specializes in cleansing, God specializes in purging, God specializes in renewing minds, God specializes in delivering, God specializes in saving souls. In this next section of the book it will be words of wisdom to encourage you, exhort you, warn you, give spiritual insight, and to edify you. Now that you know my past to the present now let's read what God will allow me to encourage you with.

CHAPTER ONE

SPIRITUAL INSIGHT

The wonderful thing I love about God is that he isn't like man. When a person does something traumatizing, then man looks to put them down and to make them a castaway. Man judges that man based off of what he has done. What God does is forgives that man, and is always looking to restore his people. Jesus came into this world not to be served, but to serve. We as a body of Christ must have the heart of Jesus. The only way you can have the heart of Jesus is to establish a relationship with him. The only way you can establish a relationship with Jesus Christ is to receive the gift of salvation. Romans 10:9 says, "That if thou shalt confess with thy mouth the Lord Jesus, and shalt believe in thine heart that God hath raised him from the dead, thou shalt be saved." Then verse ten says, "For with the heart man believeth unto righteousness; and with the mouth confession is made unto salvation." It is with your mouth and your heart that you receive the gift of salvation. It is so simple, and so many people miss it. You are justified simply because of Christ. All you have to do is confess, and then believe in your heart what you are confessing, and you are then saved.

Nicodemus visits Jesus at night in John 3:1-6. Nicodemus was a highly respected Pharisee and a member of the ruling council (called the Sanhedrin). Pharisees were a group of people who John the Baptist and Jesus often criticized, simply because they were hypocrites. So Nicodemus visits Jesus at night and told Jesus he was a teacher who has come from God. That had to mean that God was dealing with this Pharisee about Jesus, because I am sure he heard of Jesus and all the miracles Jesus was doing. So Jesus gets to the point, and takes total advantage of this opportunity to minister to this Pharisee. Jesus says, "Verily, verily, I say unto thee, Except a man be born again, he cannot see the kingdom of God." So Nicodemus didn't get this revelation, and so he says, "How can a man be born when he is old? can he enter the second time into his mother's womb, and be born?" So Jesus says, "Verily, verily, I say unto thee, Except a man be born of water and of the Spirit, he cannot enter into the kingdom of God. That which is born of the flesh is flesh; and that which is born of the Spirit is spirit." Jesus is referring to the contrast between physical birth (water) and spiritual birth (Spirit) or being regenerated by the

Spirit and signifying that rebirth by Christian baptism. The water may also represent the cleansing action of the Holy Ghost (Titus 3:5).

What Jesus was teaching to this Pharisee was being reborn spiritually, being cleansed by the Holy Ghost, being transformed, being regenerated, being born again. It is being spiritually reborn through and by the gift of salvation that will cause you to enter into the kingdom of God. There are not enough good deeds that you can do to enter into the kingdom. The enemy has deceived so many people into thinking that if they do good deeds or do nice things for people that they don't have to be saved; that is a trick of satan. I am not saying that you can't do nice things, but you can't base your relationship with God on what you do for someone. You must base your relationship with God on how you live for God. Being nice isn't good enough; being nice alone won't get you into heaven. It is receiving the gift of salvation that will get you into heaven. The world loves you based off of what you do for them, but God loves you even when you are not living holy. Living for God will cause you to forgive those who have hurt you. Living for God will cause you to love your enemies. Living for God will cause you to love people who spitefully use you. There are so many Christians who don't walk in love; they walk in jealousy and don't want to see other Christians successful. Since I have been in the church, I have seen so much. There is so much jealousy in the body of Christ and it shouldn't be like that. Being jealous, to me, is like a disease. Being jealous only hinders you from being who God has called you to be. Being jealous is a major stumbling block, and it withholds your blessings from you. If you have a problem with jealousy and you don't want to see the next person blessed, don't expect to see yourself blessed. People who are like that are selfish and are operating with the demon of pride. The Bible says in Proverbs 29:23, "A man's pride shall him low: but honor shall uphold the humble in spirit." In other words, when you are full of pride, you are looking for a great big fall. If you are lowly in spirit, or humble, then you are only setting yourself up to be blessed by God. 1Peter 5:6 says, "Humble yourselves therefore under the mighty hand of God, that he may exalt you in due time." I heard one pastor say, "You don't humble yourself just for God to exalt you." I would say you humble yourself under God's mighty hand simply because of who God is. The Bible says in Proverbs 16:18, "Pride goeth before destruction, and a haughty spirit before a fall." In other words, people who are prideful don't really confess their weaknesses and don't really want to acknowledge they need to change for the better. Prideful people judge others and look down on other people. People who are prideful never want to admit they have issues and don't want to deal with their issues. People who are like this are walking in deception and are only tricking and deceiving themselves.

That was how the Pharisees were; they were very prideful and religious and they had no real relationship with God. They walked in deception. There was a Pharisee in the Bible that said, "Lord I pray, I do this, I do that." And then there was a man who said, "Lord I am a sinner, and Lord I need you." So who do you think God honored the most? When you go to God and tell him what your issues and struggles are, you set yourself up for deliverance. But when you go to God with the mindset that you have it all together, when you know you don't, you are living in the spirit of deception. As long as you are living in the spirit of deception, then you will never be free. God knows everything anyway, because he is omniscient, meaning he knows everything about you. So you might as well be honest with God so you can be free and be blessed. People who are proud don't seek to recognize that they are dealing with pride. That is a dangerous place to be in. God revealed to me that people who are jealous are the main ones who are operating in the spirit of pride and they will never admit it if you tell them.

People who are prideful may have resentment in their heart, bitterness in their heart, hatred in their heart, and immorality in their heart. There are a lot of things or baggage that comes along with pride. The only thing that can break that type of yoke is Jesus Christ and the power of the Holy Ghost. God is love and Jesus is the light of the world. As believers, we should exemplify the fruits of the Holy Spirit. Galatians 5:22-23 says, "The fruit of the Spirit is love, joy, peace, longsuffering, gentleness, goodness, faith, gentleness, meekness, temperance: against these there is no law." The fruit of the Spirit is from the Holy Ghost. It is impossible to have the fruit of the Holy Ghost without the Holy Ghost. People that don't walk in love cannot possess the other attributes. Jesus Christ requires us to love no matter what the circumstance is; no matter what the problem is Jesus calls us to love. Jesus is the perfect example for love: Jesus was mistreated, he was beaten all night long, he was bruised, he was talked about, they accused him of blaspheme (which means irreverence or to speak evil of), they persecuted him, his own people crucified him, and when Jesus Christ was on the cross, his very words were, "Father forgive them for they know not what they do." Jesus is the perfect example of forgiving. We as believers have gone through nothing compared to Jesus.

Now let me address the people who have been hurt, who may be unsure of God and salvation, or who may have been hurt in church or by a so called believer. First, you must understand that the person who hurt you is not your enemy. The Bible says in Ephesians 6:12, "For we wrestle not against flesh and blood, but against principalities, against powers, against the rulers of the darkness of this world, against spiritual wickedness in high places." Paul is not talking about flesh and blood, but demons controlled by satan; and they are very real. The ultimate goal of satan is to destroy the church that is of Christ. So satan's job is to keep you from giving your life totally to Christ. He will use any and everyone to keep you from stepping into a relationship with Jesus Christ. You may say, "I went to church once before, and I got hurt." or "God took my loved one." or "My husband left." or "My wife left." or "I went bankrupt." or "My loved one is on crack, heroin, etc." I am telling you, even in the midst of all that, God is still God. God is not your enemy and the people who hurt you are not your enemies. The devil works through people to hurt you and to distract you. The same way God or the Holy Ghost works through people, satan does to. There is an opposing force out there that doesn't want to see you make it into heaven. Don't let what has happened to you cause you to not go to church and seek God. All though you may have been hurt in the church, or hurt by a loved one, or lost a loved one, that still shouldn't cause you to not want to try God. Sex out of marriage won't heal you or help you. Cocaine, marijuana, homosexual partner, lesbian partner, gambling, drinking, murdering, or loving money won't give you peace. None of those things will satisfy you and there will still always be something missing. Those things won't fill the void in your life or heart. The only person that can heal you is Jesus Christ. The only person that can give you joy, hope, love, peace, happiness, and self-control is Jesus Christ. The truth of the matter is that you are looking for something and you don't even realize it. Yes, you may have been molested, you may have been abused by your mate, you may be a homosexual, a lesbian, addicted to gambling, a prostitute, a fornicator, a lover of money, an atheist, a Jehovah Witness, a Mormon, or Muslim, but Jesus Christ can deliver you from all of these things. You can't let what you are going through cause you to not believe in Jesus Christ. The only way to the Father is through Jesus. You cannot get to the Father, but Jesus Christ can. Jesus Christ is the mediator between God and man and Jesus is always interceding for us.

If you have been contemplating suicide, Jesus Christ is the answer to your problems. If you are going through in a bad marriage and your spouse has given up on you, try your best to work through it because marriage is a ministry. You should never get married simply because you are lonely or for financial reasons. Marriage is something you should work at. Once you get married you become one, and the two of you are now in a ministry. The Bible says in Ephesians

5:22, "Wives, submit yourselves unto your own husbands, as unto the Lord." But so many men misinterpret that scripture because it goes both ways. In verse 21 it says, "Submitting yourselves one to another in the fear of God." Husbands must submit to their wives as well; it goes both ways. In this, Paul counseled all believers to submit to each other; for wives to submit to husbands, for husbands to submit to wives, for children to submit to parents, and for parents to submit to children. This is called mutual submission and it brings order and harmony. That is what God wants in relationships: order and harmony. The only way to properly submit to each other and have order and harmony is to have a true and sincere relationship with Jesus Christ. If Christ isn't in your home, then it is impossible to live a successful Christian life. Christianity and ministry start at home, and then move out of the home into the church, and then into the community. There is no doubt that the husband is the spiritual leader of the marriage and he is his wife's covering, and then Christ covers them, but it doesn't mean the husband is controlling or bossy. Some men take this scripture out of context. When the wife is not in agreement with what he feels he should do, the first thing one husband may say is, "I am in control, and I am the head." But God made the man head for him to be the protector of his wife, not to control his wife. The revelation to this is that Jesus washed his disciples' feet and served them, and that is what husbands are supposed to do for their wives: serve them like Christ serves his people. The husband and wife should walk side by side, on one accord, and in unity and harmony. It is hard for a husband and wife to be blessed of God if they are not on one accord and walking together. The husband must treat his wife right. The Bible says in 1Peter 3:7, "Likewise, ye husbands, dwell with them according to knowledge, giving honor unto the wife, as unto the weaker vessel, and as being heirs together of the grace of life; that your prayers be not hindered." What this is saying is that if a husband is not considerate and respectful of his wife, his prayers will be hindered. If your relationship with your wife is suffering, then your relationship with God and others will suffer. Earlier in this book, I mentioned jealousy. People who are jealous of others don't have a true and genuine relationship with God. If it was, then they would want to see everyone blessed and prosperous. You can't tell me that you have a real relationship with God when you are jealous of other people's success; it is impossible. One thing I realize is that if you serve God, and be obedient to God's Word, and rejoice off of someone else's success, then God will bless you.

You can't let what you have been through, what people have done to you, what you have lost, and what has happened to you cause you to miss out on your relationship with God. There is no one that can love you like Jesus. Look at what Jesus went through, but he still loved them. They crucified him, put crowns of thorns on his head, and pressed the thorns deep into his skull until blood started shooting out and blood was running all down his face. They beat him so bad until his flesh fell off of his body like meat, he had to carry a heavy old wooden cross, and it got so heavy that he couldn't even carry it anymore. They hung him on an old rugged bloody cross, and there were thieves on both sides of the cross. They put nails in his wrists and his feet, and he was crying out to his father saying, "Father, why have you forsaken me?" After hours of torment on the cross, and pain and agony, he gave up the ghost, or in other words, he died. Jesus died for everything you are going through. Jesus died, he was buried, and he has risen. He has risen from the dead and he is sitting on the right hand of the Father who is in heaven, and all power is in his hands. Jesus died for your suicidal mentality, he died for you abuse, he died for your divorce, he died for your addictions, he died for your flesh problems, he died for your gambling problem, he died for your drug addiction, he died for your sex problem, he died for your homosexual lifestyle. Now Jesus is alive, and we as believers can lay all of our burdens at the cross. Jesus died so that we might have the tree of life. Jesus loves us so much that he died knowing that there would still be people that would not serve him.

Now that is unconditional love. Why not try Jesus? You have tried everything else. Nothing in an individual's life will be complete until you get Jesus in it. If you notice, all the celebrities who are millionaires are still getting divorces simply because the money, the physical intimacy, and the fame can't satisfy what they really need and that is Jesus. You may tend to think that if you had a whole lot of money, your dream house, a husband, or a wife, or your dream car, that those things would make you complete. I believe it would make you happy, but only for a moment. Eventually, it will fade and start to get old. Money can solve financial problems, but if you get sick in your body, it is going to take prayer and the blood of Jesus to bring healing. The big house will make you happy for a little while; the dream car will make you happy only for a while, but that too will begin to deteriorate. I know someone that will never get old, someone who will never die, someone who will never play out, someone who is the King of Kings, and the Lord of Lords, someone that can heal you, deliver you, and set you free, give you peace, joy and happiness in the middle of a storm or crisis, and that is Jesus Christ Our Lord and Savior of the World, The Anointed One.

You may think, "What does God want with me? I am a sinner, I am a nobody, and I have done too many bad things for him to accept me." Some of you may think, "Well I want to come to him one day when I am ready, and I got to get myself ready first." I've got news for you. God is interested in the dirtiest people. Apostle Paul, for example, put out murderous threats and had the Christians severely beaten because of Jesus Christ. In Acts 9:1-17 Paul had his life changing experience. He had the Christians put in prison, but one day on the road of Damascus, he had a change that lasted his whole entire life. The Bible says in Acts 9:3, "And suddenly there shined round about him a light from heaven: And he fell to the earth, and heard a voice saying unto him, 'Saul, Saul, why persecutest thou me?' And he said, 'Who art thou Lord?' And the Lord said, 'I am Jesus whom thou persecutest: it is hard for thee to kick against the pricks.' And he trembling and astonished said, 'Lord, what wilt thou have me to do?' And the Lord said unto him, 'Arise, and go into the city, and it shall be told thee what thou must do.'" So just by him hearing Jesus speak, his life was never the same. See when you have an encounter with Jesus, your life will never be the same. This man, who persecuted the Christians, later became an Apostle who preached the Gospel of Jesus Christ, and later wrote large portion of the New Testament, defending the Gospel of Jesus Christ and died for what he believed in.

God can take a nobody, God can take an atheist, and deliver them and let them have a Damascus experience. What God is calling you to do is to have a Damascus experience. The Lord is calling your name while you are reading this book, and he is using this book to change your life so your life will never be the same. Perhaps you may think you aren't ready because you don't want to let go of that sin that you know is sin, and that you know is wrong, but you are so addicted to it until you want to hold on to it. The Bible says in Romans 8:8, "So then they that are in flesh cannot please God." So as you can see, this is a book that Paul wrote, this same man who once tore down the Christians, and now is writing about the things of God. If God can do it for him, he can do it for you. I don't care how deep in sin you are, God can bring you out. Is there anything to hard for God? Nothing is too hard for God because God can do anything. So being in the flesh is of the world, and the world is very fleshly. When you are doing worldly things or fleshly things, you cannot please God. To lie is not to please God; to hold on to the sins and baggage of this world isn't pleasing God because it is fleshly. A fleshly person cannot see the kingdom of God because in order to see the kingdom of God, you must be born again like Jesus told Nicodemus.

One thing that I didn't say earlier in this book about Nicodemus was that Jesus already knew Nicodemus' heart was ready for change. He was a Pharisee that was ready for change because he came to

Jesus at night one on one. If you know anything about the Pharisees, they were religious leaders who were hypocrites, but there was something unique about this Pharisee. The Pharisees hated Jesus and treated him terribly, but after Jesus discussed with him about being born again, his life was never the same. This Pharisee, Nicodemus, became a secret follower of Jesus. My motto for my church is, "God can change anyone that wants to be changed." If you want to change, you can change, but the only way your change can be permanent is that Jesus Christ gets a hold of you and changes you. When you get infected with the blood of Jesus, your life will never be the same. Operating in your flesh and making fleshly decisions will get you exactly nowhere in life. The Holy Spirit allowed and released me to write this book in 2007. The Lord also showed me that I was going to be not just a Pastor, and not just a traveling Evangelist, but I was also going to write books and be an author for the kingdom. God led me to write this book first about who I am, where I came from, and how I was before I got into the Ministry, and share spiritual insight based off of God's Word. I was deep in the dungeon of sin, but God took his out-stretched hand and pull me out of the pit of hell. Now he is using me for his glory. I want the adults, young adults, and young people to know that God can take someone that everyone thought would amount to nothing, and he can intervene and show the devil and my enemies that God can do anything. God is a God of the impossible. God can make the impossible possible.

What you have to realize is that *you* cannot get yourself right for God. There is nothing *you* can do to get yourself right with God; *God* is the one that gets you right; *God* is the one that gets you right for the kingdom; *God* is the one that gets you right for heaven. *You* cannot do it in your own power. If *you* could get yourself right for God, then there would have been no need for Jesus Christ to come on this earth and die on a cross. Since *you* can't change yourself, and it only takes a divine intervention or it takes the power of God to change, then you must give your life to him, and trust him with your life. Some of you may say, "Well how can I trust a God I have never seen? I have never touched him physically, I don't know what kind of cologne he wears, and I don't know where he lives. Is heaven really real?" My question to you is: How do you think you wake up every morning? Can you prove that he isn't real? Who do you think created this universe? He *is* real, he *is* alive. Look at what God has brought you out of. God has brought some of you out of so much mess, and God still loves you. So many of you may have been close to death, but God's ministering angels protected you from the death angel. What God is doing is giving you a chance now to get your life right with him before you leave this earth. God is giving you a chance to get saved before you die. The truth is that so many people think they are invincible. They don't think about the fact that they are going to die; they just live in the fast lane, make bad decisions, and then realize later that they were wrong.

There was this guy who got saved, and hours after he got saved, he died. Now my point is that you don't know when death is going to hit you. Tomorrow is not promised to you. God did not promise you that you were going to live the next day or the next year. We live by the love and grace of God and I understand that you aren't going anywhere until God says so. But what if God says it's time to go? The thing is you don't know when God is going to say your time is up on this earth, so you should make sure that you are ready and saved before he comes to take you home with him. To be honest, being in the flesh feels good; walking in the flesh feels good; but the Bible says Romans 6:23, "For the wages of sin is death; but the gift of God is eternal life through Jesus Christ our Lord." So sin only lasts for a season, and sin is designed to destroy you. So many people walk in the flesh and sin so often, not knowing that making bad decisions brings on bad consequences. So many people have died in their sin.

A kid I went to school with over ten years ago, got in a fight over a girl, and the guy shot him in the stomach and he died instantly. I knew the guy real well who got shot in the stomach because we were on the same basketball team in high school. He didn't have time to repent. I am not judging him, but if you die without knowing Christ and receiving the gift of salvation or being saved then you won't go to heaven. You cannot go to heaven without being saved. Now this guy was in the wrong place at the wrong time, and by him being around the wrong people and being involved with the wrong person, it cost him his life, and probably eternal life. When you are living for the devil, you don't have time to think about what you are doing. You don't see the results of your decisions until after you have done it. Now think about you, and ask yourself how many times you have been in situations that could have caused you to get killed, but the hand of God brought you out. I know myself; I am supposed to be dead. I don't understand everything and why God spared me, but I am just glad I was under his grace and mercy, and I love him for it. The devil is trying to take you out and he is after your soul. He knows that he can never have a relationship with God again, so he knows he is going to hell. He is trying to take as many people with him to hell as possible. You have some people that don't believe in life after death and some people don't believe there is a hell. I won't get into that type of belief because I don't want to focus on that in this book. My main goal in this book is for you to take heed to what

I am saying and give your life to Christ and for you to draw closer to God in a more spiritual and unique way.

You have to ask yourself this question: if you do believe in heaven or hell and you are not saved, where will you spend eternity? I must say that there is a heaven and hell; it does exist. I always tell my church that if you do not want to go to hell when you die, then you are ready to be saved. The only way to heaven is through salvation. Salvation is the key to eternal life, and it will cause you to unlock the door to eternal life. This world is full of people who are lost and spiritually dead. It is sad to say that there are people that are proclaiming Christianity that are still lost. You have Christian couples that are saved, but still being separated, and getting divorces. You have pastors, bishops, and leaders, who can't get along with their spouses. We wonder why the world won't come to Christ, and it is sad to say that some people in the church are doing exactly what the world is doing. The world is saying, "I don't want a God like that." What the world doesn't realize is that it is only is a trick of satan. Jesus Christ is the best example of how to live a Christian life. Once you die and stand before God, then what will your excuse be then? God is going to say, "Well you had a chance to get it right." You are responsible for your soul and you cannot base your relationship with God on how someone else is living. Even if you see that so-called believer in sin, you who aren't saved can get saved and be an example, and then possibly win that believer back to Christ. So in judgment you will be without excuse. One thing you must realize about God is that he will let you make your own decisions if you want to. God will not force himself on you; God isn't like man. When you fall short in life, God is there to pick you up, show you love and get you back on track. Man will give up on you and let you down. Man will lie on you; man will back stab you; man will turn on you. God is a God that cannot lie; he stands on the truth and he will never leave you nor forsake you. No matter what religion you are, God still won't turn his back on you. You can be a Muslim, you can be an atheist, you can be whatever, and he is still there to convert you if you want him to. Now I am not saying God accepts those religions or false gods, because they are false, but my point is that no matter what pit you are in, God is ready to change you for the better. When you get sick in your body and can't get healed, the only thing that can heal you is the blood of Jesus Christ.

Jesus Christ is the Messiah, meaning he is the Anointed One. Jesus has all power in his hands, and he and the Father are one. The Bible says in John 3:16, "For God so loved the world, that he gave his only begotten Son, that whosoever believeth in him should not perish, but have everlasting life." Now why not serve that kind of

God? That is how much God loves us, that He sacrificed his one and only son Jesus. He allowed Jesus to come on this earth and be hurt, mistreated, abused, beaten, and flogged, just so we might be saved. The sad thing about it, but this is very true, Jesus Christ died for all of humanity, but he went to the cross to be crucified knowing that all men wouldn't be saved and that there would still be people that would go to the Lake of Fire. That is why I am hoping that if there is someone reading this book that may not be saved, I hope you give your life to Christ after reading this book. Even if you want to stop reading this book right now to get saved, then that will be the most exciting, rewarding, and best decision you could ever make in your life. An individual who is not saved and living in a life of sin is gambling with their soul. You don't know when you are going to die; you don't know when the Chief Apostle, who is Jesus Christ, is going to call you on home. Trust me, when you die, you want to die in Christ. When Christ comes back, he is coming back for his church and for his people, and the dead in Christ shall rise first.

Life is like an intersection. When you come to an intersection, you have the choice to go either left, right, forward or even backwards. What you have to realize is that whichever way you wish and choose to go in life, there are consequences, and the consequences can be good or bad. That is why you need to come to Christ when you get to the intersection of life, because you may just choose to go down the wrong road at the intersection. So you need Jesus Christ to help you go down the right road. I am a very young Pastor and I was not always saved. In my teenage years, I wasn't the best person, but every now and then, I had a hunger to read God's Word. I never understood why, but I would be in my room reading the Bible. I wondered why I wanted to read the Bible. I was a dirty sinner, but I still sought after God. Now when I look back on my life, I realize that God was dealing with me the whole time, and that seed for salvation was being planted in my spirit. Now I have gone from falling to the calling. I was a wretch undone, and I made so many mistakes when I was younger, but again I went from falling to the calling. Now I am 29 years old, preaching the Gospel, pastoring, and traveling as an evangelist. Now I have become an author and I want to write books for God's people that can make them see Christ. I want people to come out of every addiction and bondage that they are in. I want people to see that no matter what type of sin they are in, Christ still wants to deal with them and transform their lives. So many sinners think that God doesn't want anything to do with them simply because of how deep they are in sin. I service notice on you that Jesus Christ is waiting for you; Jesus Christ loves you no matter what you have done. No matter what sickness you have, he still loves you. I serve notice on the devil that he has to loose you and let you go! Be loosed from that addiction; be loosed from living with that man or woman that you are not married to; be loosed from fornication; be loosed from pornography; be loosed from drugs and alcohol; be loosed from depression; be loosed from a broken heart; be loosed from an abusive marriage; be loosed from that homosexual and lesbianism relationship; be loosed from gambling; be loosed from the love of money; be loosed in the name of Jesus; be loosed. In Luke 13:10-12 there was a woman who had a spirit of infirmity for 18 long years. This segment of scripture implies that this woman was in bondage for 18 years. How many of you have been in bondage of sin for years? The Bible says she was bowed together and could not lift up herself. The revelation to this is that you are bound when you are in sin, and *you* cannot lift yourself up. That is why you have to rely on *God* to lift you up, and not try and do it yourself. When *you* try and lift yourself up, you will always make a mistake. What you have to learn to do is put yourself in God's hands; put your problems in God's hands; put that low self-esteem in his hands; put those addictions in his hands and watch your life be transformed forever. The Bible says in James 4:7, "Submit yourselves therefore to God. Resist the devil and he will flee from you." The key is that when you know you have certain weaknesses, don't put yourself in an atmosphere that you know that will cater to your weakness because you are only setting yourself up for failure.

I want to minister to some people that feel like you can never be anything in life. You may think that your life is doomed by satan based off of what you have done and you feel like God isn't there. I declare to you that it isn't over. As long as you have breath in your body and blood pumping through your veins, there is hope for you in Christ Jesus. There is a place for you in heaven; there is a place for you in the kingdom of God. The enemy wants you to focus on what you have done, what you are going through and what you think you might go through in the future based off of the choices you have made. If you put God first and seek the face of God, you will come out like pure gold. People who are not saved and don't have a relationship with God focus on what they see; they go by what they see and they are looking for things in the world to give them joy, peace, satisfaction, comfort, and love. What they fail to realize is that this world cannot bring you the kind of joy that will last. Only Jesus can bring you that joy, peace, love, kindness, and happiness that will last for eternity.

I know at times that it seems like Christ is distant from you when you are going through. Some of you may think, "Well where was God when my husband or wife left me? Where was God when my loved one died? Why am I financially unstable? Why can't I get past this addiction? Why are my loved ones suffering? Why do bad things happen to good people?" I understand that people have so many of these questions in their spirit. I must be honest: I don't have all the answers to these questions, but I do know someone that has all of the answers, and that is Jesus Christ. In the end, that is what it is all about. Jesus is the solution to your problems. I dare you to try him; I dare you to step out on faith and give him a chance. You must understand that nothing happens without God knowing about it. In this world, you will have trouble because sin entered into the world through the first Adam. As a result of sin, death entered into the world. That is why we need to make sure we continue to live for God. Those who aren't saved need to get right with God so you can see your Christian loved ones again.

2Timothy 3:12 says, "Yea, and all that will live godly in Christ Jesus shall suffer persecution." So in this epistle, Paul is telling Timothy that if you are going to be a Christian, you will suffer persecution. Persecution is to cause to suffer for belief. In becoming a believer, there are things that you will have to do simply because of the Gospel of Jesus Christ. I must tell you this because there are many Christians who were babes in Christ and went back into the world simply because they were not properly disciple. What you have to realize is that once you get saved, then the devil is going to attack you harder because the devil wants your soul. He wants you to not make it into heaven. I have heard so many new believers say, "Since I have gotten saved, it seems like I am going through more. When I was in the world, everything was better." That is only a trick of the devil to make you go back into sin and bondage. You must understand that to whom much is given, much is required. Being a Christian is a major responsibility and it is and can be challenging at times, especially when you are going through and being attacked by the devil. That is why you as a believer must stay in God's Word. The Bible states in 2Timothy 2:15, "Study to show thyself approved unto God." You must not be surprised when people criticize you, hurt you, or misunderstand you simply because of your belief in Jesus Christ and living for Jesus Christ. You can even look for your family to misunderstand you and not fully believe in you. The devil will attack you through your family only to seek to distract you. The enemy will use people to tell you that you don't need to go to church that much or you don't even have to go to church at all to be saved or to go to heaven. Oh, you will hear that one a lot. However, if I am not mistaken, I believe that the Word of God says in Hebrews 10:25, "Not forsaking the assembling of ourselves together, as the manner of some is; but exhorting one another: and so much the more, as ye see the day approaching." In other words, we must be among our brothers and sisters in Christ. Some may say, "Well, you don't have to go to church to do that." Well, what you must realize is that you are the church and God has put worship buildings on this earth called churches. You should be in the house of God so you can get edified, built up and encouraged so that you can go out and fight the enemy. You can't get strength to fight the devil sitting at home. The purpose of church is to encourage each other, revive each other, minister to each other, and pray for one another. It is important that you go to church because as we get closer to the day when Christ will return (no man knows when that will be), we will face many spiritual struggles, and even persecution, for what we believe in.

I have so much respect for one young lady at the Columbine shooting. One of the shooters shot her and she died for Christ. How many of you are willing to not just die for Christ, but how many of you are willing to die in Christ? Are you willing to give up your addictions and bad habits? One thing you don't want to do is to die without Christ because of the works of the flesh. That addiction isn't worth you missing out on heaven. If you are reading this book right now, I encourage you to repent and give your life to Christ. If you have fallen away from God, I encourage you to come back to him. If you are saved but not growing, I ask you to repent for being complacent and lazy and renew your commitment to Jesus. You can just read a chapter a day in the Bible and meditate on that chapter. You can learn a verse every week and meditate on that verse until you get it in your spirit. What you have to realize is that the Antichrist is going to grow and the enemy is going to literally use that to keep people from professing Christianity. As a believer or one who is seeking God, you should never make excuses for not going to church. So many people in the world say they don't want to get saved or come to church because hypocrites are in the church. Well there are hypocrites in the world too. You can't let how you see other people act dictate whether or not you want to serve God. It is not so much what you see hypocrites do; it is really whether or not you are willing to let go of your fleshly lifestyle to walk in the fullness and knowledge of God. Once you stand before God, you will not be able to tell God, "Well I didn't get saved because there were hypocrites in the church." God may just say, "Well you shouldn't have let that cause you to not to live for me." Yes, there may be hypocrites in the church, but a person shouldn't use that as an excuse to stay in sin. Once you stand before Jesus Christ in the judgment, then you will be without excuses. Now that you are still living, you have a chance to give your life to the Lord. Once you die, it is over. You can't expect to live any kind of way and think you will still go to heaven.

It doesn't work that way. In order to make it into heaven, you have to be born again. You have to surrender your whole entire will and life to God.

I understand that some may say, "Well, do I have to be perfect to be a Christian?" No, you don't. You will still sin and make mistakes. The Bible states in Romans 3:23, "For all have sinned, and come short of the glory of God." Sin in the Greek is 'hamartia', which means fault, offence, or trespass. What you have to realize, is that some sins seem bigger than other sins because of their obvious consequences that are much more serious. For example, killing a person seems worse than telling a lie or hatred; adultery seems worse than lust. My point is that all sins make us sinners. No matter what the sin is that we commit, it still separates us from God. Your sin may not seem as bad as the next person's sin, but you are still being cut off from God. You must understand that no matter how deep you have been in sin, no matter how much sin you have committed, Jesus still wants a relationship with you. What you must realize is that you will never be perfect and you will always make mistakes. That is where you get into grace, mercy, and repentance. Once you become born again, you have that chance to be able to repent. Even with the Holy Ghost in you, even with being in right fellowship with God, you will still make mistakes. What I know is that when people act like they are more holy than everyone, God has a way of humbling you. Our job is to restore a person that has sinned and not look down on them. If you have a true relationship with Christ Jesus, you will restore and not judge. One thing my best friend and I talked about was that some people see others who do more obvious sins and look down on them and put them down simply to try and not focus on the baggage that is in their lives. The Bible says in Galatians 6:1, "Brethren, if a man be overtaken in a fault, ye which are spiritual, restore such a one in the spirit of meekness; considering thyself, lest thou also be tempted." No Christian should ever think they don't need other believers because we all need each other. What Paul is saying in this verse is that if a person is caught in a sin, the person that is in right fellowship with God should not look down on that person that committed the sin, but that person that is spiritual should show love to that sinner who fell, and minister to him in love, in meekness and with pure and clean heart. Now Paul says right after that to watch yourself or you also may be tempted. I would like to put it like this: the person that is spiritual and restoring the sinner, that spiritual person should be careful too because he is subject to fall into sin as well, and will fall into sin at some point in time; then that spiritual person will need restoration as well. I can say it like this because I have been there so many times. No one is perfect and we all fall short to the glory of God. If a person that is proclaiming Christianity sees a person fall into sin and they put that person down in rage, anger, and judgment, then that person only shows that they have no true relationship with God. They are only deceiving themselves. Jesus was picked at, ridiculed, lied on, talked about, and accused of being the devil. These people said the Son of the Living God was demon possessed and Jesus still forgave them, still showed them love, still ministered to them and sought to restore them. That is why if a Christian is putting you down based off of what you have done and not trying to restore you, then something might be going on with them.

As a believer, I have experienced so much and I have been hurt by so many people, but I have kept the faith and forgave the many people that hurt me and turned their backs on me. Many people thought I wouldn't make it, but while man said no, God said yes. I was deep in the dungeons of life, but I know a Savior that will reach down in the dungeons of life. I know a Savior that can take you from the pit to the palace. I know a Savior that can and will bring you out of the pit of darkness and transform your life like never before. I went from falling to the calling and as I look back on my life, I sometimes wonder how in the world I got to where I am today. I can say boldly today that God has called me to do this work because I wasn't trying to be in the ministry. When I got in church for real, I was just a pew warmer and I got no playing time in the church. As God continued to cause me to work on my spiritual game, I started to work out spiritually by getting into the Word, praying like never before, and seeking the face of God. Then God showed me that, "Tommy, I am ready for you to come off of the pew. I am ready for you to come off of the bench because you are ready to start. You have a game to play. I want you to preach the Gospel to this nation. I want you to pastor." Have I been perfect along the way? No. Have I made mistakes along the way? Yes. However, his grace is sufficient. His grace and mercy was extended to me. Thank God. What a wonderful Savior. Jesus is the King of Kings and the Lord of Lords. No matter what we do, he is still there to love us.

One of the things God showed me is that he has to know he can trust you with a gift. It is easy to get prideful when you know you have a gift, but God doesn't give you a gift to make you look good. God gives you a gift because he wants to get the glory out of his people. God works through man to get a message out to his people. So your gift isn't just for you, but your gift is for someone else. Before promotion, comes the test. Jesus was led in the desert and was tempted by satan. Now if Jesus ever experienced an attack while being on this earth, that one was a real attack. In Matthew 4:1-11,

Jesus was hungry because he fasted for forty days and forty nights. Jesus was tired and hungry, but yet he still passed the test. Because he passed the test, he was promoted. Now suppose if he would have not passed the test, then we would be in trouble. The Bible indicates that he was sinless; he was without sin and he was perfect. Jesus went through many different things during his ministry, but he fought the good fight of faith and he put on the whole armor of God. Jesus worshiped God by the way he lived on earth and he poured into other people's lives. God showed me that your worship to God initiates God to reveal the manifestation of his presence in your life. In other words, when you worship God in spirit and in truth, he will reveal himself to you. When you are worshiping God, you are only setting yourself up for God to show himself or reveal himself to you. You cannot be in your flesh when you are worshiping God. Flesh is of the flesh, and spirit is of the Spirit. The flesh goes against the will of God, and the Spirit does the will of God.

Your praise causes God to abundantly pour out his blessings in your life. When you reverence and respect the Lord for who he is, you are praising him and giving him the glory and the honor that he deserves. When you find yourself going through in life, just praise God. Just praise him with your lips and praise him with everything that you have. I will tell you two powerful weapons against the enemy and these two weapons will also draw you closer to God. Those two weapons are prayer and worship. God loves it when you pray and worship him. Worship will get his attention and prayer will cause him to reveal himself to you. Praising God is reverencing him for what he has done. Worship is thanking him for who he is. Who is he? He is the Son of the Living God; he is the Christ, the Messiah, and the Anointed One. Prayer causes God to draw closer to you. That is when you get to know God for who he really is and you begin to develop that one-on-one relationship with God. I understand that you may have issues and problems, but you may be like the woman with the issue of blood in Mark 5:25-34. She had this disease for twelve long years. Now, can you imagine bleeding like this for twelve years? One text says that she spent all she had going from doctor to doctor. That is how people are today. They have issues, they are depressed, or they are suicidal simply because they spiritually have the issue of blood. What you are doing is you are looking for people to accept you; you are looking for love in all the wrong places. If you are in a marriage where you are not happy, God is saying I am ready to heal you. God is saying I want to deliver you. God is saying I want to set you free. God is saying I want to give you peace, joy, and happiness. Perhaps you are in a marriage where when you first met your mate and in the beginning, he/she was the love of your life. Now, years later, they have become your worst nightmare and you are somewhat resentful towards your spouse. You're holding on to unforgiveness towards them and you somewhat hate them. You want to leave them, but you are afraid to step into the unknown. God is saying to you today to pray for your spouse. If you submit to God, then it will be easy for you to work out your marriage, if you want to work it out. You cannot effectively love other people if you do not love your spouse. Don't deceive or trick yourself. If you are not being who God has called you to be in marriage, then it makes it difficult to love other people. What God wants to do is to use the issues of life to draw you to him. The Bible says in James 4:8, "Draw nigh to God, and he will draw nigh to you." It is just that simple; come near to God and he will come near to you. Seek God and God will come for you because he loves you just that much.

As I was stating earlier, God has gifted each and every one of you with a unique gift from heaven that God gave you even before birth. The Bible says in 2Timothy 1:6, "Wherefore I put thee in remembrance that thou stir up the gift of God, which is in thee by the putting on of my hands." Now you must realize and understand that it is not *your* gift, it is the gift *of God*. It comes from God and belongs to God. Your gift is not to bring *you* the glory, but you are gifted to bring glory to *God*. No matter what sin you are in, you are gifted. You are called and you are chosen of God. God wants to be a part of your life, so make him a part of your life today. You are too gifted to be defeated. God has laid his hands on you and he wants to stir up your gift for the use of his kingdom. Perhaps you don't know what your gift is and you don't know what your calling is. I didn't know what my gift was. I thought I was gifted to play basketball, but that wasn't my true gift. Once I got saved and gave my life to Christ that is when I started to find out what my true gift and calling was. When I started walking with the Lord and I totally surrendered, God showed me that I was called to preach the Gospel of Jesus Christ. He didn't show me right in the beginning because it probably would have scared me. As I started to mature and grow in God, then he showed me. Later on, after I started preaching, which was a couple of years later, he showed me I was called to Pastor. I realized I was called to pastor while I was at NC A&T State University in Greensboro, North Carolina. All of a sudden, I just didn't have a desire to be there anymore. I had a desire to go to Bible College and learn of God's Word. I was going to go to a Bible college in Atlanta, Georgia, but God shut that door. I was glad and my friend James Brown helped me to look for other Bible colleges. We happened to be on the internet and we found a little old Bible college called John Wesley College in High Point, North Carolina. I already felt in my spirit that I was called to preach and Pastor. When I looked at the different majors and I saw Pastoral Ministries as a major, boy my spirit just rejoiced. God showed me that was where he wanted me to be. I went there and I graduated on May 6, 2006. Now I am in seminary working on my Masters of Divinity at Shaw University Divinity School. My purpose for being in seminary and wanting more knowledge of God's Word is so that I can be effective. One thing I do realize that I must emphasize is that there are things that seminary can't teach you that only the Holy Spirit can teach you. However, I am just hungry for God's Word and I yearn to know his will for my life. So when I started to grow in God that is when I realized I had a gift. That gift is to preach the Gospel to the nation. If you would have told me eight years ago that I would be pastoring, traveling and preaching, I would have thought you were crazy. However, God has a way of getting a hold of you.

Your gift does not dictate who you are, but it is your relationship with God that determines who you are. Your gift doesn't make you. There are a lot of people that are gifted and talented, but they possess no integrity. It is our relationship with Jesus Christ, our Savior that makes us. So many people tend to get prideful because of the gift that only God could give them. They lose sight of what their true assignment is. Our true assignment is to win souls to the kingdom of God and bring glory to God by doing the will of God. The manifestation of your gifts does not determine how anointed you are. Your relationship with God is a requirement which increases your anointing and it also gives you the victory. The more you draw closer to God, then the more he anoints you for service. In you seeking God for who he is, he then knows that he can trust you with any assignment that he gives you to fulfill on this earth. The gift is in you only to bring God the glory and not to bring you glory. It is in you establishing a close relationship with God that he anoints you the more. Because of that, it also gives you the victory. A person that is anointed has the spirit of meekness; a person that is anointed walks in humility. When the enemy starts to come against them, they rely on the source, which is Jesus Christ. No matter what state they are in, they still have the victory.

CHAPTER TWO

IF I CAN JUST GET THROUGH THE ROOF

– Mark 2:1-5 –

Sometimes it seems like the pressures of life just get the best of you, but God is always setting you up to get what he has promised you. The Bible says in Genesis chapter 15, where God made a covenant with Abraham, that when God makes you a promise or a binding agreement, you can look for God to give you what he has promised you. That is why you cannot look at what you are going through and think it is always going to be like this. Your change is coming. I have never seen a storm that has stayed. You are going through; you are just passing through the trial to get to where God is trying to take you. No matter what your physical eyes may see, no matter how you feel, you will make it through. No matter how hard things may get, you are going to make it through the test. You will pass the test if you submit to God, resist the devil, and draw near to God.

In Mark 2:1-12, we have a situation of four individuals and one sick person who are desperately trying to get to Jesus. These four men had faith in Christ that would be considered as crazy faith. These gentlemen had the kind of faith that could move mountains. The Bible doesn't indicate anything about these four men other than the simple fact that they did a great deed for this paralytic. This paralyzed man could not help himself, but God sent him help. That is what God will do for you if you will allow him to. He will always send you help if you want it. When you activate your faith in Jesus Christ, God will always send you help. Some of you are going through things right now. What you are going through seems like it is just beating you down, but God is going to send you help. The enemy is trying to cause you to not have faith in your Savior, who is Jesus Christ. When you don't have faith in God, then you are telling God that you don't trust him. The Bible says in Hebrews 11:1, "Now faith is the substance of things hoped for, the evidence of things not seen." You cannot see faith; you cannot touch faith; you cannot smell faith; but just because you can't see, smell, or touch faith, doesn't mean you shouldn't use it. In Hebrews 11:6 it states, "But without faith it is impossible to please him: for he that cometh to God must believe that he is, and that he is a rewarder of them that diligently seek him." The word 'diligently' in the Greek means to search out, crave, demand, and seek after. So you have to crave God, and want God. In you searching for God, looking for God, studying the Word, praying, and going to church, then you are showing God you have faith in him. When you don't trust God, then you are only proving that you don't have faith in God.

These four men were concerned about this paralytic man's situation. The Bible doesn't indicate about where these men came from, what their race was, or what their culture was. The thing these four men did for this paralytic was a Christian deed. There may be things that are taking place in your life right now and they don't make sense to you. You may be wondering, "Why is this happening to me? Why me? Why am I going through this?" I am sure this paralytic man was wondering why he was in this condition and why he was like this, but God linked him up with some faith-filled men. You may be wondering why the enemy is attacking you in this world you are living in. You may wonder why when you get out of one problem, then another problem pops right back up. The Bible states in Romans 8:28, "And we know that in all things work together for good to them that love God, to them who are the called according to his purpose." So you must know and understand that even in the midst of your storm, you still have purpose. You may be sick in your body, but you still have purpose. You may be sick with an illness, but you still have a work to do. By loving God in the midst of your circumstances and problems, you are only showing God that you love him and trust him. Whatever you are going through won't last forever. There must be an end to your problems eventually. You must understand that God is all-knowing. He knows the beginning from the end. God knows how many times you will mess up and when you will mess up, but his grace is still sufficient. You can really learn something the four men in Mark 2:1-12 who carried this paralyzed man. What you can learn from these men is that no matter what you see with your natural eyes, God can change any and every situation. You can see the gift of faith operating in these men's lives. Mark 2:1 says, "And again he entered into Capernaum after some days; and it was noised that he was in the house." This means everyone knew he was there. When Jesus is in the house, then something miraculous is going to happen, if you have the faith and believe that he can do it. You must give Jesus something to work with. The thing you must give him to work with is your faith. When Jesus is in your life, you can look for great things to happen for you. Now it doesn't mean that because Jesus is in your life that you won't have any problems.

It does mean that when Jesus is in your life he will give you the peace, joy, love, and happiness that you need while you are in your storm. As a matter of fact, the more you get God in your life, then the more you become a threat and a target for satan. He knows that once you surrender totally to God, then you will no longer be an asset for him.

Mark 2:2 says, "And straightway many were gathered together, insomuch that there was no room to receive them, no, not so much as about the door: and he preached the word unto them." So the only way these four men could get this man to Jesus was by going through the roof. Sometimes you have to go through the roof of your issues and problems to get to Jesus. Sometimes you have to go through the roof of depression to get to Jesus; go through the roof of no faith to get to Jesus; go through the roof of drugs and alcohol; go through the roof of molestation; go through the roof of abuse in order to get to Jesus; but you must be willing to go through whatever is holding you back from God to get to God. These people came to hear Jesus preach. Jesus knew what their motives were, but yet he still preached to them. Jesus knew they came for many different reasons, but yet Jesus used their motives, good and bad, as an opportunity to preach the Word to them. Mark 2:3 says, "And they come unto him, bringing one sick of the palsy, which was borne of four."

The devil may be fighting you on every side and you may be going through a test, but just be like these four men. You just need to get through the roof. Sometimes you just have to spiritually bust through the roof to get what God has for you. Bust through depression; bust through low self-esteem; bust through verbal and physical abuse; bust through homosexuality; bust through fear; bust through drugs; bust through lesbianism; bust through promiscuity. Tell yourself, "I am about to bust through!" Mark 2:4 says, "And when they could not come nigh unto him for the press, they uncovered the roof where he was: and when they had broken it up, they let down the bed wherein the sick of the palsy lay." Jesus saw their faith and this man received his healing. Now obviously, this paralytic had faith in Jesus too because he got his healing. The Bible says faith without works is dead. These four men could have had faith all day, but if they would not have acted on what they believed in their spirit, then that man would still be paralyzed. For some of you who are reading this book, God has promised you a business; God has given you an idea or ideas; God has promised you to be wealthy and healthy. I tell you to go through the roof and to believe God and act on what God has promised you. It is not going to come to you. You have to go for it. Success isn't going to come to you. You have to go for success. Some of you are so gifted and God has blessed you so much. Please don't let your dreams or your gifts go down the drain. Get connected with Jesus and go all the way. Tear the roof off and run to Jesus, so you can walk into your destiny and purpose. This paralyzed man had faith as well. I can imagine when they picked him up. They could have been ministering to him saying, "Man, today is the day for your healing. Jesus is in town and he is preaching in a house in our town. We know that Jesus can heal, deliver and set free, and he will heal you today." I can imagine the paralytic got pumped up and said, "Let's go! Take me to Jesus so I can get my healing!" That is how you have to be. You have to walk in faith and have works behind your faith. Bill Gates got a vision before he started it. He worked the vision. When you have a vision, you have to be willing to work it so it will manifest to where you can see what you believed all the while.

CHAPTER THREE

YOUR SUFFERING WON'T LAST FOREVER

– Romans 8:18 –

There are some of you who are reading this book and you may be going through some type of suffering. Paul says in Romans 8:18, "For I reckon that the sufferings of this present time are not worthy to be compared with the glory which shall be revealed in us." There is a price for serving Jesus Christ. There are going to be things that you will have to endure for serving Jesus Christ, but in the end the reward is great and you will receive an eternal reward. Paul mentions the suffering that Christians must face. For 1st century believers, there was economic and social persecution; some even faced death. We also, as individuals in this 21st century, must face trials for serving Jesus Christ. Even though we as Americans are in a free country, we must not take Jesus for granted. In other countries, people are dying for Jesus Christ. The Christians in America can't even get to church on time. You must understand that you as a believer are not going through anything compared to what Jesus went through while he was on earth; enduring his trial and going through a horrendous crucifixion. I encourage all of God's people to know that your suffering won't last forever. Being that you are in this fleshly body, you will tend to think that what you are going through will continue to last. I declare in the Holy Ghost that there is always a shifting out of your problems. I have never seen a storm that has stayed. It might last for a couple of hours; it might rain for days or weeks at a time; a tornado or a hurricane might show up every now and then; but it has to cease. It cannot stay. It may seem like the weights of life are just beating you down. What you have to realize is that this world is in confusion. Due to the fall of man, this world became imperfect and corrupt. (Genesis 3) Through man, sin entered into the world. Confusion entered into the world through the first Adam. So if you understand that concept, you will then understand that storms are a part of life. However, it is through God's Holy Word that he helps you and teaches you how to endure bad situations that rise up against you. Paul says in Romans 8:18, "For I reckon that the sufferings of this present time are not worthy to be compared with the glory which shall be revealed in us." In the Greek, 'suffering' is 'pathema' which means hardship, pain, or affliction. So if Paul is indicating in this area of scripture that there are sufferings, then that is something we can't get around. However, the storms, hardships, pains, and problems of life don't dictate or control who we are in Christ. Just because you are going through, doesn't mean you are defeated. What makes you defeated is when you throw in the towel. You have come too far to throw in the towel. It's not over yet. You are destined for greatness. Your sufferings are for you to grow and to mature in God. What you are going through is only designed to draw you closer to God. The enemy thinks that what you are going through is going to make you give up on God and have a lack of faith, but the more you go through, the more you need to draw closer to God.

I must state that the very things you are going through are only for God's glory to be revealed in your life. The God we serve will wait until your situation gets so bad and you will think he has forsaken you and then that is when he will reach in and pull you out of your terrible situation. I hope you have read the beginning of my book where I told you about my life. If God can do it for me, he can definitely do it for you. I thought God had given up on me, but he was only strengthening me and my character. Here I am in my twenties preaching, pastoring, and evangelizing. My goal is to travel the nation preaching God's Word. There is one thing you cannot do when you are going through and that is faint. If God's Word says that your present suffering are not worth comparing with the glory that will be revealed in you, then that means God's glory is greater that what you are going through. I don't care what you are going through, you can have a selfish mate, you can have a mean mate, and you can be sick in your body even at the point of death; God's glory can and will be revealed in your situation and life. You may be discouraged based off of what you are going through, but the devil wants you to look at what you are going through and he wants you to think that the Son of the Living God won't shine on your behalf. The Son is always shining, but I want to encourage you and tell you that after the stormy clouds in life, the Son will always show up and show out on your behalf. This Son I am talking about came in human form through a Virgin Mary (Matthew 1:18-23), and is fully God and was fully human. This Son I am talking about cast out devils, healed the sick, raised the dead, healed lepers, and healed the lame. This Son I am talking about hung on a bloody, dirty, nasty, smelly, old rugged cross with two thieves on it. After all of that, this Son said, "Father, forgive them, for they know not what they do." This Son I am talking about is the Son of the Living God who was beaten all night long for us; who was mocked, talked about, back stabbed, mistreated, spit in his face, denied his divinity; but through all of this suffering this one man went through, he never denied God, who is his Father, and he never denied his purpose. That is how God is calling us to be; that no matter what we go through in this life, we will never deny God and never deny our purpose based off of what we go through.

We can look at Jesus' life and see how he endured suffering and he never once complained; and he was fully human as well. What God wants to do through the believers and through people who are saved and have confessed Jesus as Lord and Savior is to bring about revelation of his glory through his believers. The very thing that you are going through, satan thinks it is going to defeat you. He thinks that bad marriage is going to defeat you; he thinks that abusive husband is going to defeat you; he thinks that alcoholism is going to defeat you; he thinks fornication is going to defeat you; but the devil is a liar. You are coming out with the victory. Through your sufferings God's glory is still going to be revealed in your life. You have to declare to the devil that he has attacked you long enough and that you are sick of your addictions, you are sick of life beating you upside the head, and fight back with your spiritual weapons. Fight back with worshiping God; fight back with prayer; fight back with faith; put on the whole armor of God. It talks about the whole armor of God in Ephesians 6:13-18. Paul is instructing you on how to fight with your spiritual weapons such as putting on the helmet of salvation. That is an important one because you must be saved in order to defeat the enemy. To kick the devil completely out of your life, you must get saved and give your life over to Jesus Christ, so you can have a helmet to put on.

Another important spiritual weapon to have against the enemy is the sword of the spirit, which is the Word of God. Without the Word of God, you cannot be successful against the enemy's schemes. With the Word of God, you can make it through anything that the devil throws your way. When the devil throws trials and tribulations your way, just get down on your knees and pray. Pray in your spirit and bow down and worship the Lord and it will begin to confuse the enemy. The devil isn't omniscient (knowing everything) like God is. The devil is so one-track minded until he thinks that when he hits you with certain things, then that will defeat you. What he doesn't realize is that you are more than a conqueror in Christ Jesus. He doesn't understand why you won't give up based off of what you are going through. His ultimate task against believers is to attack them and make them give up on God. So I don't care what you are going through, don't give up on God. If you're reading this book and you are not saved, I encourage you to give your life over to Jesus Christ before it is too late. Tomorrow is not promised. The key to defeating satan's attacks is to draw closer to Jesus so you can have peace in the midst of your attacks from the devil. "Weeping may endure for a night, but joy cometh in the morning." (Psalm 30:5) You may be going through right now and you may be having a night experience, but there has to come a time in your life, if you keep the faith, where you will start to have joy in the morning. Morning doesn't have to necessarily be an A.M. time, but your morning can be whenever God wants it to be. You must understand that the sufferings are small and short, but the glory in Christ Jesus is everlasting and eternal. If what you are going through is short, then that means the glory that is going to be revealed *to* you, has also got to be revealed *in* you. God is going to show your enemies and the devil that God's glory lasts forever and that the sufferings are for a short time. So if the glory is going to be revealed in you based off of what you went through, then that means you will become a partaker in the glory of God that is to be revealed. Now that you have been through and suffered, God says he can reveal himself to you. So if you stand on that hope that the glory of God is going to be revealed *in* you and *through* you, then that means what you are going through right now is a stepping stone for God's glory and his goodness to be revealed in you. In order for his glory to be revealed in you, then that means you have to be a Christian. Someone that is not saved will never smell the aroma of God's glory. A person that is not saved will never understand the old bloody and rugged cross. Someone who isn't saved doesn't know the glory of God and doesn't know the significance of his blood.

At the cross is where you lay all of your mess and everything you have ever done to displease our Savior. That is why it is important that you give your life to Christ because you cannot save yourself. Once you get saved and give your life to Christ, you still won't be perfect, but you are covered with his blood and your life will never be the same. I dare you to try Jesus; I dare you to make him your Lord and Savior. If you are saved, I dare you to go to the next dimension in your relationship with him. The glory in you right now is greater than what you may be going through right now. The revelation to this is that you can have the glory of God in you right now while you are in the middle of your sufferings. It may seem like there is no glory being manifested in your life, but having faith in God in the middle of your sufferings will reveal to you the glory that has been in you the whole entire time. So how do you know you have the glory in you while you are suffering and going through? You will know you have the glory in you while you are suffering when you won't faint on God; when you won't give up; when you will fight and say, "God, I am going through this thing right now with the right attitude. God, it seems like you are distant from me based off what I am going through, but God, I am still going to trust you no matter what." That is how you know you have the glory of God in your life. The catch to that is while you are constantly going through, God is allowing you to go through, just so you can see that his glory is in you in the middle of you going through. God is with you right now as you are reading this book. The Lord is speaking to you and ministering to you right now as you read this book. My goal in this book is to speak to your heart and to warn you, encourage you, and give you hope for your life. The thing about it is, you may be going through or may have been through the fire and through the storm, but you won't ever know how strong you are until you go through the suffering. When you go through, that only shows how strong you really are. Now that you have been through a lot and have been in some 'should have been dead' situations, now you know there is a Savior; now you know how strong you are. It was nothing but the hand of God that brought you up and over. There are only some things you are going through that are setting you up for maturity.

In Genesis 39, Joseph was attacked by Potiphar's wife. Because of the God in him, he didn't commit adultery with Potiphar's wife and he was thrown in prison. He was tested and went through, but it only made him stronger and matured him. In Acts 16:16-25, Paul and Silas were imprisoned because Paul cast out a demonic spirit from a girl who was predicting the future. The men who were making money off of this little girl could no longer make money from her simply because she got free from this spirit. Just because Paul did this, he and Silas got beaten and were put in prison. They went through this difficult time. My point is that even though they were in prison, the Bible says that they prayed and sang praises to God. What God is calling you to do is when you start to go through, and while you are going through, be like Paul and Silas and start praying and singing praises unto God. When you start to pray and sing unto the Lord, something eventually is going to happen. God has to move on your behalf. Even in your mistakes and sins, it will still work out for your good. Just because you make a mistake or slip up and sin, it doesn't mean you don't love God. The Bible says in Romans 3:23, "For all have sinned, and come short of the glory of God." Even while you are a Christian, you will still make mistakes because that is life. We are in this corruptible flesh, but when you do make a mistake, know that you have a Savior that you can talk to about anything, and you can repent. You will sin daily, even being a Christian, but you can't let your sins and your mistakes keep you from drawing closer to God.

What the devil wants to do is to condemn you for your sins, but the Holy Spirit brings conviction, and conviction brings upon repentance, and condemnation brings guilt. God wants you to be convicted so you can repent and change. When you sin and make mistakes in life, God expects you to learn from them, repent, and seek to draw near to him. The sins you commit should not cause you to give up or go away from God. So many people sin and they fall away from God simply because they think God is mad with them. God loves you. God loves you so much that he gave his one and only Son, Jesus Christ, just for you. God will never stop loving you. Even when you stop loving yourself, God still won't stop loving you.

I remember I used to think God didn't love me because of all I had done, but as I started to seek God and grow and mature, I realized how much he does love me. It is in your mistakes and sufferings that you should realize how weak you are and how much you really need God. People, who are going to be successful in God, as far as their relationship with him, must realize that they are a sinner saved by grace. Grace is unmerited favor, meaning you have done nothing to get it; it's just given to you by God simply because he loves you. One thing I realized is that some believers, who are prideful, look down on other believers who are struggling in their walk with God and they judge them. The Bible says in Galatians 6:1,

"Brethren, if a man be overtaken in a fault, ye which are spiritual, restore such a one in the spirit of meekness; considering thyself, lest thou also be tempted." Usually, the ones who are looking down on other believers who are struggling are the ones with baggage in their lives as well. We only should use our mouths to restore and not put down. The devil wants what you are going through to sabotage your faith in Christ Jesus. There is someone out there that may feel like giving up, but don't throw in the towel. Jesus is the answer to your problem; only he can give you peace while you are going through. If the enemy can get you to forfeit in your walk with God, then he knows you are already defeated. The devil is jealous of you because you can have a relationship with Jesus Christ and he can't. It's over for the enemy; he is doomed to the Lake of Fire. What he wants to do to you is make you suffer so much so you can give up and faint. You shall reap the wonderful blessings from God if you faint not. I don't care what you are going through, I don't care what it looks like, please don't give up on God. There comes a time that things will get better in your life. It may seem like what you are going through is getting worse, but you have to fight the devil in the spirit. The Bible says in 2Corinthians 4:17, "For our light affliction, which is but for a moment." In other words, your troubles and your issues should not diminish or cause you to lose your faith. What you are going through, to God, is a light affliction. Your suffering won't last forever.

CHAPTER FOUR

STRETCH OUT YOUR HAND

– Mark 5:25-34 –

In this story, you have a woman that was bleeding for twelve long years. She was in desperate need of a Savior. She was in desperate need of Jesus Christ. She was subject to bleeding for twelve long years. Some of you may be going through some things right now, and you are wondering how in the world you are going to get out of it. You may have experienced some things in the past and even now, and it seems like your destiny is crippled. I say to you that it isn't over for you. Your destiny may be delayed, but it is not denied. You may have experienced some things in the past that have crippled you, but I don't care what your situation looks like right now, you still have hope. As long as you are still living and have blood flowing through your body, then there is still hope. Even in hopeless situations, you still have hope. The Bible says that there was a certain woman who had an issue of blood for twelve years. She went from doctor to doctor, and she spent all she had, but she still didn't give up. I know that you may have had the same issues, same problems, or same addictions for years, but don't let your issues of this life keep you from getting all that God has in store for you. The enemy will use your issues against you to make you feel like you are not worthy of what God has for you. You may have committed a crime, felony, been on drugs or on drugs now, or have so many bad habits, but I encourage you that you still have hope. That hope you have is in Jesus Christ. Once you give your life to Jesus Christ, then all of your sins, he remembers them no more. It is as if they are cast into the sea. When you throw something into the sea, more than likely it will drown. That is what God will do for you; he will drown your sins and he will forget all about them.

We all have weaknesses and things that we battle and deal with, but God's grace and mercy protects us and we are covered with the blood of Jesus. God wants you to learn from your mistakes. So many people keep making the same mistakes and never learn from them. You would think that after a while they would get the picture and see that their mistakes in life are causing them to get nowhere in life. If you keep making the same mistakes, then you will keep getting the same results. If you renew your mind, then you will get better results. (Roman 12:2) So many Christians can't grow in God or get to the next dimension or level, simply because they won't change their way of thinking.

This is what the woman with the issue of blood did when she heard of Jesus Christ; she changed her way of thinking. There has to be a shift in your mind for the better before you can start making the right decisions. The only way that there can be a shift in your mind is for you to give your life to Christ. Only God can change your mind for the better; only God can renew your mind for the better. So many people are so blind to their problems and issues until they can't even get anywhere in life, simply because they won't renew their minds. Immediately, when this woman with the issue of blood heard of Jesus, her mind was renewed and she believed in Jesus Christ. This woman's faith was extraordinary because she did what she had to do to get to Jesus. All it takes for you to get to Jesus is repentance, believing he is the Son of God, confessing with your mouth, believing it in your heart, and you are saved. (Romans 10:9) At this time, it was so hard for this woman to get to Jesus. Yet she still pressed. My question to you is: Are you willing to press your way to Jesus? Are you willing to let go of the things of this world, and that are of the flesh, in order to get to Jesus? God has made it so easy for us to get to Jesus by him sacrificing his one and only Son just for us.

This woman with the issue of blood had a change in her mind. She had suffered many things of many physicians, and had used up all of her resources for this cure, and still could not get her healing. Some of you are suffering or have suffered many things for many different reasons; you may have been or are under attack by the enemy, but I encourage you to be like this woman with the issue of blood and just stretch out your hands to Jesus. When you stretch out your hands to Jesus, then that shows God that you have faith in him that he can do anything he wants to do. I understand that it can be difficult for some people to trust in a God they have never seen, smelled, nor touched, but you have to have faith. It takes faith to believe in God. Faith is believing in those things you cannot see. I understand that it is hard to trust in God when you have done things your way all of your life, but I dare you to try him. If you try Jesus, I promise you he will come to your rescue. You have tried everything else, why not try Jesus? You have nothing to lose, but much to gain when you seek his face. This woman with the issue of blood suffered many things of many physicians; meaning she went from doctor to doctor. It was unlawful for her to be around anyone with this type of condition she had, but she didn't let her condition keep her from getting to Jesus. She knew that once she got to Jesus, she wouldn't be in that condition any longer.

Jesus wants you to come to him just like you are. He wants you while you are the dirtiest sinner, the messed wretch undone. He knows that he can wash you with his blood and he knows that he can change your life forever. I can testify to that because when I got serious about Jesus, my life was never the same. People said I would never make it and didn't think I was going to make it, but Jesus believed in me the whole time. Look at me today. If Jesus can bring me out, he can bring anyone out. I am so glad that he saved me while I was young. I know in the end I won't regret it. Many of you have heard of Jesus; even if you overheard people talking about him or someone actually tried to minister to you. Since you are reading this book and now that you have heard so much about him, will you stretch out your hand in faith and give Jesus your heart totally? For you believers, will you recommit and surrender your all to the Almighty Savior and begin to go forth in ministry? How bad do you want to know Jesus in a personal and intimate way? I promise you, Jesus won't beat on you; Jesus won't lie to you; Jesus won't lie on you; he won't back stab you; he won't hate on you; he is not jealous of you; he won't cheat on you; he will love you unconditionally and he wants to deliver you from the bondage of sin. Is that one night stand worth you missing out on heaven? Is that relationship you are in, that you know isn't Godly and it isn't going anywhere, worth you missing out on heaven? Is that excessive alcohol and drugs you are addicted to worth you missing out on heaven?

This woman with the issue of blood suffered for many years. There are some of you that may have suffered and may still be suffering. Some of you may not even know you are suffering, but your suffering isn't there to destroy you. Your suffering is only to bring about Godly maturity in your life. The suffering this woman went through brought her straight to Jesus. She had spent all she had, so there was nothing left for her but Jesus. That is where a lot of people are today; they have tried everything in this world and it only brings them temporary satisfaction. That is all the world can do is bring you temporary satisfaction. Drugs, alcohol, marijuana, homosexuality, lesbianism, fornication, pornography, and gambling can only bring you temporary satisfaction. It is only a weapon of the devil to keep you in bondage to these things I just named. I know a man name Jesus Christ, our Lord, who can give you permanent satisfaction. He can give you peace while you are in the most terrible storm in your life. A lot of people are at the point in their lives where their only hope is Jesus Christ. That is why the Lord led me to write this book, so you can realize that Jesus wants to deliver you and set you free. He wants you to walk in liberty. It is the name of Jesus that makes demons tremble. Jesus Christ, whether people want to believe it or not, has all power in his hands. Being that we are in this terrible world, it seems like God isn't here, but I must tell you that God is still in control. In Christ Jesus we have hope no matter what environment we are in. God is omnipotent, meaning all powerful.

This woman with the issue of blood was in a 'should have been dead' situation, but the God of Abraham, Isaac, and Jacob kept her from this traumatizing situation. How many people have done everything they knew they could do, and really deep down within they are ready for change, but just don't know how to go about it? One of the first steps to changing is that you have to admit that you have problems. The enemy has so many people deceived about their problems. You have to admit you need to change and admit *to God* that you need to change. Once you admit that you have a problem, you then set yourself up for change. This woman with the issue of blood knew she had a problem, and she went to Jesus for the cure to her problem.

God is looking for sincere believers that will stretch out their hands to Jesus. God is looking for that sinner to stretch out their hands to him so he can clean them up and make them whole. God wants to make you whole today. God wants to restore you. God wants to change your way of thinking and God wants to better your attitude. This woman with the issue of blood got worse instead of getting better. What you have to realize is that sometimes before God moves, things will get worse instead of better. That is so God can show up and show out. When she had heard about Jesus, she came up behind him in the crowd. Now this woman was willing to go through the crowd to get her healing. That was an act of faith. Sometimes people have to be willing to go through the crowd to get to Jesus. She came up behind him in the crowd and touched his cloak or garment, and immediately her bleeding stopped. Once you come in contact with Jesus, your life will never be the same. This woman with the issue of blood came in contact with Jesus and her life was never the same, simply because she had faith. If you want to get God's attention, then walk in faith. Faith in God causes God to respond to you. Faith in God causes God to reveal or show himself to you. Jesus says, "Who touched my clothes?" The disciples said, "Jesus, look at all these people that are around you. It could have been anyone that touched you Jesus." The revelation to this is that so many people can say they are believers, but only the ones who worship him in spirit and truth will get his attention.

When you worship him in spirit in truth Jesus will say, "Who touched me?" Jesus will say, "Someone touched me with their faith. Someone touched me with their worship. Someone touched me with their obedience." Jesus kept looking around to see who had done it. Then the woman, knowing that Jesus knew, turned around and worshiped him. She came and fell at his feet trembling. I can imagine she was crying; somewhat afraid, but happy at the same time. She told him what happened and Jesus told her that her faith had healed her. The revelation to this is that the power was not in the garment Jesus had on, but the power was her faith. By her having faith in Jesus, she stretched out her hand. Go ahead and stretch out of your bondage; stretch out of that addiction. You are too big for it. You can't fit that low self-esteem anymore; you can't wear it. You can't fit that depression anymore; you have outgrown it. You can't fit that suicide anymore. You can't fit those addictions anymore; you have outgrown it. Go ahead and get something that fits you just right and that you will never outgrow. That is Jesus Christ. You can fit him; you will never out grow him. The more you suffer, then the more you need to seek God. The more you go through life, then the more you need to seek God. God uses the experiences in life to shape and mold our character.

When you find yourself out in the wilderness and having been pulled out of Egypt, then all you have to do is be like the woman with the issue of blood and just stretch out your hand to Jesus Christ. In stretching out your hand to Jesus, then it shows that you have faith in God for him to handle your situation. Some of you may be believers and may be strong in the Lord, but it may seem like the weight of the world is just beating you down. It seems like this and that happens, but God is only setting you up for victory. Your place of suffering only qualifies you for maturity in God. What you have to realize is that every storm, situation, or trial that you go through, is only making you stronger in the Lord. "Be strong in the Lord, and in the power of his might." (Ephesians 6:10) When you are strong in the Lord, you can make it through anything that the enemy throws your way. For I consider that our present sufferings are not worth comparing with the glory that will be revealed in us. So all of the things you are going through right now are only setting you up for what God has for you, if you obey his word. Now notice, you have to obey God's Word. If you want what God has for you, then you must serve him with your whole heart. You cannot partially serve God and expect to receive what God has for you. That means God's glory is even going to be revealed in your suffering.

You may wonder how what you are going through is going to cause God's glory to be revealed in your life. Everything you are going through or have been through is only designed to draw you closer to God. When you love God in the midst of your problems, issues, difficulties, bad situations, short comings, faults, doubts, and fears, it will only cause it to work out for your good, simply because you love God no matter what is going on in your life. Can you love God under pressure? Can you love God when things are not going your way? Can you love God when your bills are due? I can imagine this woman was crawling and just fighting her way through to get to Jesus because she knew that Jesus Christ was her only hope. Are you willing to crawl towards Jesus? Are you willing to do what you have to do to seek the face of God? Are you tired of living the same old lifestyle that is getting you nowhere in life, but keeping you in bondage?

This woman was very weak and had no strength, but in her weakness she made her way to God. What you have to know is that when you are the weakest, that is when you need to draw closer to Jesus. You may be weak in your relationship with God, but if you can only get to Jesus, you will receive your strength from him. Some of you who are reading this book may be leaders in a church, but you may be or have been spiritually weak. You may be in the choir or on the praise team, but you are still spiritually weak. God has come to strengthen you and all you have to do is just stretch out your hand to Jesus so he can make you whole. This woman with the issue of blood had so much faith in Jesus until she didn't even have to hear Jesus speak a word. She knew from a touch of her Savior that she would be healed. Can you still have faith in God when he doesn't move when you want him to move? So many people are impatient and can't wait on God. God's timing isn't like our timing; when you get impatient, you will make a lot of wrong choices in life. Do you have enough faith in Jesus to get you everything you need spiritually? God is much more interested in making sure you are whole spiritually than making you rich financially. "Seek ye first the kingdom of God, and his righteousness; and all these things shall be added unto you." (Matthew 6:33) When you seek to draw closer to God and not serve him simply for the blessing, but serve him for who he is, then God will bless you simply because you have a sincere heart. Everyone can't handle success; it takes having a relationship with God to handle success. That is why you hear about all these rich people who are not believers getting in trouble, getting divorces, and killing each other simply because they have God nowhere in their lives. Now God doesn't mind you obtaining what is on this earth; he doesn't mind you having great wealth; but when what is on this earth and the fame and things of this world take your focus off of God, then that becomes a major distraction.

This woman's faith in God got her exactly what she needed. What you have to know is that your faith in God will get you exactly what you need from God. If you are hurting, then look for God to heal your heart. If you are depressed, then look for God to make you no longer depressed. If you have any type of addictions, then look for God to restore you. He will do it if you allow him to. Everything that God is allowing you to go through is only to teach you about faith in him. He wants you to see and know that he was with you the whole entire time, even in your sin, and even right now. I don't care what state of mind you are in, God is with you. God is everywhere and you cannot hide from God. He is God all by himself.

All God is waiting for you to do is stretch out your hands in faith to him and believe that he has everything you need. I know you may be going through right now or have been through, but just stretch out your hand to Jesus. Your marriage may be on the road to divorce, you may be divorced, separated, sick in your body, depressed, on drugs, but just stretch out your hand to Jesus and he will see you through. You may have zeal and a hunger for ministry, but stretch out your hand to Jesus. Going into ministry will not happen overnight. Becoming a preacher won't happen overnight. You might say, "Well

I am on fire and I have zeal." Well zeal outside of God's timing will hurt you. Zeal without wisdom will hurt you. Preaching the Gospel is very challenging and difficult. It requires you to spend a lot of time in the presence of God, studying God's Word, and seeking the face of God. Some preachers today don't want to study, don't want to spend time with God, and they just want the title, but don't want the relationship with God. You may believe God for your loved ones to get saved, but just be like the woman with the issue of blood and stretch out your hands to Jesus in faith. When the devil is fighting you on every side and it seems like your situations are getting worse, then just stretch out your hand in faith. Stretch out your hand in prayer; stretch out your hand in worship to God. By you having faith in God, it only ignites your anointing and gives you the victory and power over every demonic force that would want to come against you. When you have faith in God, it only improves your relationship with God. When you don't have faith in God, it cripples your relationship with God. Be like the woman with the issue of blood, and stretch out your hands. No matter what, continue to seek the face of God.

CHAPTER FIVE

IT'S TIME FOR YOU TO CLEAN YOUR HOUSE

– Matthew 21:12-17 –

So many people in this world allow any and everything to come into their house. Later, I will tell you what I mean when I say 'house'. You may figure out what I mean when I say 'house' as you continue to read. What you have to consider is that the choices you make and the things you do can either bless your house or corrupt your house. Now let me go ahead and give you the revelation of what I mean when I say 'house'. You may have thought I was talking about where you live as far as a residence, but when I say 'house' I am talking about you; your temple. "What? Know ye not that your body is the temple of the Holy Ghost which is in you, which ye have of God, and ye are not your own?" (1Corinthians 6:19) Many people think they have the right to do whatever they want to with their body. You must understand that once you become a Christian, the Holy Spirit comes to live in your body and you are to no longer live the way you want to live. God knows what is best for you. Jesus Christ's death freed you from the bondage of sin, so now you are bought with a price.

When you are using someone else's belongings, you try to do everything you can to take care of it because it belongs to someone else. That is how it is in the spiritual; you don't belong to you; you don't own you; God owns you. You must take care of what belongs to God. What is it that you are allowing in your spirit or heart that you know that God is telling you to release and give it over to him? The very thing you are holding on to in your temple, in your body, in your spirit, is killing you spiritually. You know God is telling you to release it, but it is so appealing to your flesh until you can't shake it. God is saying to you right now to shake it off of you before it defeats you and causes you to miss out on your ultimate destiny. What I have discovered is that so many people today walk in the flesh more than they walk in the spirit. "This I say then, Walk in the Spirit, and ye shall not fulfill the lust of the flesh." (Galatians 5:16) Live by the Spirit, and you won't gratify sex out of marriage, you won't gratify drinking alcohol, and drugs, or addictions. "For the flesh lusteth against the Spirit, and the Spirit against the flesh: and these are contrary the one to the other: so that ye cannot do the things that ye would." (Galatians 5:17) What Paul is describing here is that the two forces are in conflict with each other. Paul is not saying that these forces are equal because the Holy Spirit is infinitely stronger. He is just saying that they are in battle towards each other and obviously the Spirit will win because it is of God. You cannot try to follow the Holy Spirit by your human effort because you will fail every time. The only way you will make sound decisions and walk in love towards everyone is to be full of the Holy Spirit. Being full of the Holy Spirit will help you to walk in love and will help you to be slow to anger. If you are easily offended and easy to anger, then that is a major problem. Someone with the Holy Spirit is slow to anger, isn't full of jealousy, isn't full of self, and isn't prideful. They are full of joy, full of love, full of self-control, full of patience, full of gentleness, full of kindness, full of goodness, and full of faithfulness. (Galatians 5:22-23) When you are not walking in righteousness, you cannot expect to grow and mature in God. It doesn't matter if you are a leader in the church or whoever; if you are not walking in obedience to God's Word, then you cannot come into the knowledge of who God really is. The only way that you can come into the knowledge of who God is, is that the Holy

Spirit reveals it to you. In this story, where Jesus cleans the temple, there are some spiritual issues going on. Number one, these people are sinning in God's house; they are sinning in God's temple. This was to be a house of prayer; the house of God. That is the purpose of your temple of your body; it is supposed to be a temple of prayer, a temple to worship God. These people are in a place where God dwells, but because they are so deep in sin, they are not even aware of God's presence. What I have realized is that when you are so deep in sin, you cannot even sense God's presence in your life or in the atmosphere. That is how it is today; you have people who have access to the Word of God, they have a church, and they are even cognitive enough to know what is right and what is wrong, but they don't have that spiritual cognition going on for them to realize that they are not in God's presence.

They were in the temple, but the temple was not in them. While they were in God's temple, they were corrupting their own house or temple by what they were doing in the temple. These people in the temple were buying and selling there, they were gambling in the house of God. That is what people are doing in God's church today; they are in church, but they are corrupting their temple or house, which is themselves. Your house, which is you, is the temple of the Holy Ghost. Jesus overthrew the tables of the money changers and the seats of them that sold doves. The Greek word for money changers is 'kollubistes', which means coin dealer.

Are you selling yourself out spiritually for something that is of the flesh and for something that can cause you to miss out on eternal life? They were in the temple and they sold and bought; they were gambling in the temple of God. Are you selling your temple to the things of this world? Is it worth you missing out on what God has for you? Jesus overthrew the tables of the moneychangers and the seats of them that sold doves. He was not angry to the point of sin, but he was cognitive of the fact of what the temple of God was for. That is why you should get in the Word of God, so you can know what your temple or your body is for. The purpose of God creating you is for his use and for his glory. This was the second time Jesus cleared the temple. (John 2:13-17) Now I must say again, I am not talking about where you live or your residence, but I am talking about you as a person. What are you putting into your temple? What are you putting into your body that is displeasing God? What are you allowing into your spirit or your mind? Anything that is not of God that you will allow into your mind and spirit, it can have a negative effect on you spiritually and maybe even physically. People who grow up and murder people, they just didn't decide they would grow up and kill somebody, it was things that happened little by little that caused them to do that particular sin. Is something that is an illusion worth you missing out on eternal life or going to heaven? An illusion is only a misconception; a misconception is something that you interpret incorrectly. When you are walking in the flesh, it is only an illusion. You think that walking in the flesh will get you what you need. If walking in the flesh is a sin, which it is, then it has to be a misconception. If it is a misconception, then that means you are interpreting it in the wrong way.

Jesus says to them, "It is written, My house shall be called the house of prayer; but ye have made it a den of thieves." (Matthew 21:13) This quote that was said by him comes from Isaiah 56:7. The blind and the lame came to him in the temple and he healed them. This verse goes right into saying what Jesus did after he cleaned out the temple. Are you willing to let Jesus clean up your temple? If Jesus cleans up your temple, your life will never be the same. There are so many people in this world that are spiritually blind. They are blind and they don't know that satan is their enemy. He is using people every day to do his work. I have also discovered that there are a lot of spiritually blind people in the church. There is a major attack on the church. The devil's ultimate task or goal is to destroy the church. So many churches are being shut down and falling simply because the church is being hit from their blind spot by the enemy. You as a mature believer need to be there for the people who are struggling spiritually. We are our brothers' keeper. For the ones who are not saved that are reading this book, now is your chance to give your life to Jesus Christ. If you die in your sins, then heaven will not be your home. You must be born again; you must be saved in order to make it into heaven. Being a good person won't get you into heaven. It is having that relationship with Jesus that will get you into heaven.

Right after Jesus cleans out the temple, he then begins to do miracles in the same temple that was corrupt. So the revelation to this is that you can have done so much sin in your temple, and God can come in you, clean you up, purge you, and use you for his glory and his glory alone. God takes messed up temples and renovates them for his use and for his purpose and then makes the devil out to be a liar. No matter what kind of lifestyle you are in, God can clean you up and use you. I am a prime example of what God can do. I was on my way to hell, but God stepped into my life and changed my life for the better. Now he is using me for his glory and for his people. In other words, God takes people who are messed up and who seemingly seem to be difficult for change and God takes them, and renovates their minds, renovates their hearts, and uses them for his glory. The enemy wants you to think that there is no hope because of the sin you are in or because of what you see. You have to tell the devil that what you see isn't the end result. You have to cut the enemy with the sword of the Spirit, which is the Word of God. You have to declare that you are more than a conqueror in Christ Jesus. Though your situation may look bad or unchangeable, you still have to stand on what God's Word says for your life.

"And when the chief priests and scribes saw the wonderful things that he did, and the children crying in the temple, and saying, Hosanna to the son of David; they were displeased." (Matthew 21:15) Hosanna, in the Greek, means adoration. A revelation God gave me to this verse for his people of today is that when God cleans you up, when he renews your mind, delivers you, saves you, fills you with the Holy Ghost, calls you into the ministry, and exalts you, then you can expect some people to be jealous and indignant towards you; even people in your own family. There are always going to be people that will not receive you. Even Jesus' own people didn't receive him, so you can expect some people not to receive you as well. The enemy will use people who are closest to you to keep you from serving God and getting saved. One thing God showed me is that you have to be willing to be delivered from people to get what God has for you. Your main deliverance can also be from people. When God begins to transition you for the better, then everyone won't like that. When God begins to take you to deep depths and higher heights in God, then everyone won't like that; and that is just a part of life. There are also people out there that will be happy for you and love you for the steps you are taking and making to serve the Lord. God will always place people in your life that will help you to grow and to mature in God. It is in God transitioning you for the better that will cause your enemies to be exposed.

When Jesus was ministering, and when he came on the scene, it showed who the Pharisees and Sadducees really were. Jesus exposed them for who they really were. They claimed to love God, but they never accepted the ministry and life of Jesus Christ. The chief priests and scribes were indignant and full of jealousy. They were prominent leaders who were much respected, but they were still envious of Jesus, all because Jesus had done what was right. When they heard the children crying out to him, they really got jealous. Jesus is so powerful that he can even reach out to little children. It doesn't matter what age you are, you can still receive Jesus Christ as your personal Lord and Savior. Jesus was so powerful during his earthly ministry simply because he stayed connected to the Father. God wants us to stay connected with him so we can keep our power; not to bring glory or to edify us, but to keep us who God wants us to be on this earth and to do effective ministry on the earth.

CHAPTER SIX

GOD WANTS TO GIVE YOU PEACE DURING YOUR STORM

– Mark 4:35-41 –

In our lives, we all go through many different changes and challenges in life, but it is in the challenges in life and difficult times that cause us to see who God really is to us. God doesn't allow us to go through things just to make us have pain. He allows us to go through knowing that trouble won't last always. "For our light affliction, which is but for a moment, worketh for us a far more exceeding and eternal weight of glory." (2Corithians 4:17) Our afflictions to God are light. He knows that while we are going through, he is there with us. What you have to realize as a believer is that storms are a part of life. There will be some things in life that you will just have to go through. That is why it is important that you get saved because you don't know the future. You don't know what you will face tomorrow. You don't know when your time is up on this earth. Since you are living here in this imperfect world, there will be things that you will have to go through. You cannot pass a storm without having to go through it. You can get an umbrella or put on a raincoat when there is a storm and rain. You can be in your car with the windshield wipers on with all of the windows rolled up, but you still have to go through the storm. Just because you are a believer, it still won't stop you from going through a storm.

For some reason, it seems like when you were not saved that everything was going okay, but the moment you gave your life to Christ, then it seems like everything wants to happen for the worse in your life. That is only a trick of the devil to make you go back into the world. The devil is just jealous because you gave your life to Jesus. Satan is our adversary or an accuser of the brethren. Be self-controlled and alert. Your enemy, the devil, prowls around like a roaring lion looking for someone to devour. (1Peter 5:8) When you are under attack or going through a storm, you may be weak. So in that attack, look to draw from other strong believers, stay diligent in prayer, and seek the face of God. Satan is always looking for someone to devour. The devil wants to disconnect you from God. That is what sin does; it separates us from God. He doesn't want

God's people to step into relationship with him, so he will throw all of your weaknesses at you and seek to tempt you in every area where you are weak to try and capture you back into the world. The devil doesn't mind you coming to church, singing on the choir, singing on the praise team, working in the church, and even knowing scripture. He knows scripture, but he uses it in ignorance.

The moment you start to pursue holiness, integrity, and righteousness to God then you automatically become a threat to his kingdom. The enemy sees now that you are pursuing holiness and sanctification, setting yourself apart to righteousness, and trying to live for God the best way you know how. Then he seeks to throw all your familiar sin back in your face to bring you back into bondage. I am here to tell you that God wants to give you peace in the middle of your storm. I don't care what it looks like in your life; God wants to give you peace in your storm. Yes it may look dark; you may be in a tunnel of bad situations; but there is light at the end of every tunnel. "When the enemy shall come in like a flood, the Spirit of the Lord shall lift up a standard against him." (Isaiah 59:19) In Job, the purpose of Job was to demonstrate God's sovereignty and the meaning of true faith. Job had true faith. Everything that Job went through, when he lost his children, his money, and got sick to the point of death, he still didn't give up on God. In the end, God gave him back more than what he had before. You can look at that as a test. Job passed the test. He was tried on every side, but Job didn't let what he went through cause him to give up on God.

You may be under some type of attack, but the devil cannot destroy you. God wants to give you peace in the middle of your storm. God wants to give you peace in the middle of your abuse. He wants to give you peace in the middle of your depression. He wants to give you peace in the middle of your financial situation. He wants to give you peace in the middle of any situation you find yourself in. No matter what the problem is that you have, Jesus wants to give you peace. If you are or have been suicidal, Jesus wants to give you peace. "And the same day, when the even was come, he saith unto them, "Let us pass over unto the other side. And when they had sent away the multitude, they took him even as he was in the ship. And there were also with him other little ships. And there arose a great storm of wind, and the waves beat into the ship, so that it was now full. And he was in the hinder part of the ship, asleep on a pillow: and they awake him, and say unto him, Master, carest thou not that we perish?" (Mark 4:35-38) It may seem like Jesus is asleep while you are going through, but just when it gets really bad, then it will wake him up and he will give you peace while you are going through. What you are going through is only a test of your faith. In this life, you have to be tested; Jesus was tested just as we are. (Matthew 4:1-11) Some of you have been through so much in life until it has made you tired and stressed out, but God is saying that if you hold on, he will make you better. You may think your situation or your storm is so bad and it seems like you are alone, but you are not alone. Jesus Christ is with you while you are in the middle of your storm and he wants to give you peace.

"And there arose a great storm of wind, and the waves beat into the ship, so that it was now full." (Mark 4:37) The Greek word for storm means whirlwind or squall, which is like a bad hurricane. Your storm may be like a whirlwind, but God is saying that there is nothing too hard for him that he cannot fix. No matter what your problems or your storms are, he is going to get the glory out of what you are going through. I know it seems like the devil is winning, but he is not. The devil is a loser and God has never lost a battle. All odds may seem to be against you and you have been petitioning God or praying the same specific prayer for days, weeks, months, and even years, but God's timing is not like man's timing. God doesn't move according to when we want him to move; he is divine and Spirit. God knows what you can handle and what you cannot handle. If you are going through it, then he knows that you can handle it. Look at all that Jesus had to go through during his earthly ministry. After all he went through he still sacrificed his life for us because he knew that he was the only one who could redeem us. I know this may sound strange, but sometimes you need to thank God for some of the storms in life. Some storms in your life are to draw you closer to God.

In this storm with his disciples, Jesus taught them a lesson about having faith in the middle of a storm. Sometimes God will allow you to go through the storms in life to increase your faith and to draw you closer to him. There was a woman who was crippled for 18 years. She would go to the synagogue every Sabbath and hear Jesus teach. One particular Sabbath, Jesus called her forward and Jesus laid his hands on her and immediately she was healed, and she glorified God. (Luke 13) Her going to hear Jesus teach showed that she had faith in him. It was her faith and in her hearing the Gospel being preached that got her healing. "Faith cometh by hearing, and hearing by the word of God." (Romans 10:17) When you continue to hear the true Word of God and the Gospel of Jesus Christ, it will increase your faith in God. The more you hear the Word, then the more your faith will increase in God. The Greek word for faith is 'pistis', which means assurance or reliance upon Christ for salvation. As you can see, there is a reason why faith is stated so much in the Bible. It is linked to Jesus; in order to believe in Jesus and believe that he is the Son of the Living God, you must have faith.

These disciples had faith in Jesus Christ which is the reason why they called on him in the middle of this storm. They may have demonstrated a lack of faith based on the situation they were in, but they had faith in Jesus to call on him in the middle of the storm. That is how you have to be; you have to call on Jesus in the middle of a storm. You may demonstrate a lack of faith based on your storm, but make sure you call on the name of Jesus and seek the face of God while you are in your storm. Believe that God can strengthen and give you peace in the middle of your storm. "And he was in the hinder part of the ship, asleep on a pillow: and they awake him, and say unto him, Master, carest thou not that we perish?" (Mark 4:38) The Greek word for perish is 'apollumi', which means to destroy fully, meaning they would have been wiped out. The storm was so great that the boat was nearly swamped. Your storm in life can be so bad until it seems like it has swamped you or has almost destroyed you, but the storm you are enduring is only a test to mature you in God.

The storm was so bad until the disciples lost hope based on what they saw. That is why, as a believer, you cannot go by what you see. If you are not a believer, you cannot go by what sin you are in and think that God has given up on you. God wants you just like you are. He will change you. You have to go by what God says and walk in faith. When you begin to walk in faith of God's Word, then your change will eventually come. I am telling you by experience. When I first started serving God, it was really difficult and I made a lot of mistakes along the way. However, I was honest with myself and I was honest with God. Then little by little, I felt in my spirit that I was getting stronger and stronger in the Lord until other believers started noticing it as well. It may seem like one storm is coming after another, but you have to hold to God's unchanging hand because your change is on the way. There is nothing too hard for our Lord and Savior Jesus Christ. From a theological perspective, Jesus was sleep, meaning in the Greek, he was resting; he was asleep, and the storm had an effect on the disciples, but it didn't have an effect on Jesus. There is nothing or no kind of storm that can hinder Jesus from bringing you out. Now Jesus was fully human (incarnate, meaning having a bodily form), but yet it still had no effect on him. He was sleep in the midst of the storm. That indicates that he was God in the flesh and that he had total control over nature itself. The storm had no effect on him and he was comfortable in the midst of the storm. He could have or might have slept in the storm because he wanted to teach his disciples about trusting and having faith in him.

It may seem like Jesus is sleep while you are in your storm; you keep praying and you have believed God for so long and he still hasn't answered you yet. Maybe God is trying to birth something out of you like faith, patience, ministry, or a business. We are living in a world that doesn't want to be patient and doesn't want to do ministry. God has gifted you; he has given you some type of ministry gift and he wants you to utilize it in the body of Christ. It may seem like you have been going through for so long and you are about to lose hope, but God wants to give you peace in the middle of your storm. God is with you in the middle of your storm. Although Jesus was asleep in the middle of the disciples' storm, he was still there with them. Jesus went out into the boat knowing that there would be a storm, but he still went and others went with him as well.

When you are in a storm in life, Jesus is willing to walk right in it with you. You may think that your storm is so bad and God is not with you, but God is right there with you while you are going through. He is there to strengthen you in the middle of your storm. Jesus might have fallen asleep in the middle of the storm to test the faith of the disciples and to stir up prayer in their lives. In believers today, their prayer life is so weak. People in the church are falling away because of a lack of prayer life. When the disciples were tested, their faith seemed weak because they feared what they saw with their natural eye, which was the storm. God is calling you to not lose faith based on what you are going through in life. You believe God for many different things and there is nothing too hard for God. Just make sure that what you believe God for is according to his will. If it isn't according to his will, then you will not get it from God. So many people want to do things before praying. Then they get in trouble and then want to rely on God. "Pray without ceasing." (1 Thessalonians 5:17) Jesus was asleep, but he wasn't asleep. "He will not suffer thy foot to be moved: he that keepeth thee will not slumber. Behold, he that keepeth Israel shall neither slumber nor sleep." (Psalm 121:3-4) So although it seems like God is asleep in your storms, he really isn't asleep. His heart is awake. God was physically asleep in the boat with his disciples, but his heart was awake. God knew what was about to happen and he knew that he was using this storm to mature his disciples and teach them about faith and prayer. In the middle of the storm, they trusted Jesus. They went immediately to him in this storm and this showed that they had faith in Jesus to handle the situation.

Some of you who are reading this book may have been in situations so bad until it seemed like you didn't know who to call on. Be like these disciples; when your situation gets so bad and it gets beyond your control, then that is when your faith has no choice but to rise to the occasion and you begin to call on the name of Jesus and trust in God with all of your heart. Although the disciples' faith seemed weak based on what they saw, they were somewhat strong simply because they believed that Jesus could solve their problem and he did. They had their Master with them; their Lord and Savior. That is the kind of confidence as a body of Christ that we have to have. No matter what storm comes your way, no matter what difficulty is in your life, you have to have confidence in the Master and believe that he can and will give you peace in the middle of your storm. I know it is hard and you have endured so many storms in life; you have been hurt, misunderstood, let down, lost some things, lost loved ones, but through it all, God wants to give you peace in the middle of your storm.

"And he arose, and rebuked the wind, and said unto the sea, 'Peace, be still.'" (Mark 4:39) The wind stopped after him rebuking it. In other words, Jesus spoke to nature and nature obeyed. That proves that God is in control of nature, God is in control of the universe because he created this world. (Genesis 1:1-31) "And he said unto them, 'Why are ye so fearful? how is it that ye have no faith?'" (Mark 4:40) I believe the disciples had what it took to go through the storm. Jesus knew that because he said, "how is it that ye have no faith?" I want you to know that I believe in every reader that reads this book; saved or not saved, I believe in you. For the people that are not saved, I believe in you that you will get saved after reading this book. For the ones that are saved and have fallen away, I believe in you that you will get up on your feet, and come back to the Lord. God wants you to have peace in the middle of your storm. I don't care what you are going through in your life; Jesus is the antidote for your storms. Jesus is greater than any storm you will ever face, so rely on him so he can speak to your storm.

CHAPTER SEVEN

YOU CAN ATTACK ME, BUT YOU CAN'T DESTROY ME

– Genesis 37:1-36 –

I understand that some of you are in situations right now that don't look so good, but you are only going through what you are in because it is a test. You are being set up for greatness. You are being set up for your destiny. You are being set up for everything that God has in store for you. Some of you believe God for certain things and there are certain things you want to accomplish in life. There are certain things in your life that you want to see come to pass, but trying to make things happen in life for you outside of Christ is not a good place to be in. You don't attain true success until you have found out who the successor is, and that is Jesus Christ. I must warn and tell you that you must be careful who you share your dreams and visions with because there are dream stealers. There are people out there in this world that are very indignant like the religious leaders were. Everybody doesn't want to see your dreams and visions come to pass. In Genesis 37, this man named Joseph had dreams and visions that his own brothers didn't want to see come to pass, simply because of jealousy and indignation.

Some of you have a terrible past and have been through so much in life, and now you are trying to live for God and go forth in your future, but it seems like the more you try and live for God, then the harder it gets. It is only an attack from satan because he sees and knows how awesome your future is going to be in the Lord. I must state that the enemy can attack you, but in the name of Jesus Christ, he cannot destroy you. There are some times that the more you live for God, the more people who are familiar with you want to bring up your past and use it against you. The Bible declares in 2Corinthians 5:17, "Old things are passed away; behold, all things are become new." What I have realized is that all the enemy has against the believers who are now living for Jesus Christ is their past. In essence, he really doesn't have that because God remembers your sins no more and your life is turned over to him. This man named Joseph had a major calling on his life, but he had to go through a lot before he could be used of God. One thing God showed me is that there are no shortcuts in ministry. When God has specifically called you to preach, pastor, or evangelize, there is no shortcut to it. You have to go through the process in which God wants to take you through. Although Joseph was gifted, anointed, and appointed, he still had to be taught of the Lord. The enemy attacked him at a very young age, simply because of the call that was on his life. God knew that this young man would help his family and bring his family together in the end. Even though Joseph went through a lot because of his brothers being jealous of him, God still turned it around for Joseph's good.

What I have realized is that jealousy is a powerful weapon the enemy uses against God's people. It is sad to say, but jealousy is on people's jobs, in people's families, in people's marriages, in people's relationships, and it is also in the body of Christ. Joseph went through all of this hardship and pain in his life all because of jealousy. Jacob's name was later changed to Israel, who was the father of Joseph. Joseph brought back the evil report of his brothers. Israel loved Joseph more than all his children, because he was the son of his old age. He made him a coat of many colors. Joseph's brothers saw that their father loved him more than all his brothers and they hated him and could not be nice to him at all. So that means they were always being unpleasant towards him. Joseph started to dream dreams, and he told the dreams to his brothers, and they hated him even more. I must state again that you should be careful and prayerful of whom you tell your dreams and visions to because there are people that don't want to see you succeed in life. By him telling his brothers what God gave him, it caused him to get thrown into a pit, and from the pit to slavery. What his brothers didn't realize was that through it all, even though Joseph had a bragging problem in the beginning, God's hand was still on him.

Some you who are reading this book might be in a pit, but just know that God's hand is still on your life and you will come out pure as gold. What God is going to do is use your pit experiences in life to bring you out of the pit. Joseph went from being his father's favorite to being thrown in the pit by his evil brothers. From the pit, he was sold into slavery in Egypt, where Pharaoh resided. The Egyptians didn't even acknowledge the God of Israel. You must know that when the Lord is with you, then it doesn't matter what negative things come into your life, you will still be able to find peace in it. Joseph knew he was in God; he found peace while he was in slavery in Egypt. You can be in prison and still have peace, if you have the Lord with you. I understand that many of you are going through different things and you are in some Egypt-like situations, but God wants to give you peace while you are in them. Many of you are going through certain things right now, and you are wondering when it is going to be over, but God is trying to teach you something while you are in your storm. Many of you may be in a pit right now, but God is about to give you joy while you are enduring your storm.

When Jesus was in the garden of Gethsemane, he was at the end of his earthly ministry, and he prayed and relied on God for strength. Joseph would tell all his brothers what dreams he had and that just made them hate him even more. What I have realized is that you can tell the wrong people what God is doing in your life, and that can cause them to dislike, envy, or even hate you even the more. It would seem like since you are telling people that God is blessing you with this and that, they would be happy for you, but in reality, some people are not happy for you. Joseph's brothers hated him all the more because of his words and dreams. If you look at the New Testament, you will find out that the more Jesus would preach, teach, and do miracles, then the more the religious leaders hated and envied him. So as you begin to do what God has called you to do, walk in destiny and purpose, and continue to do God's will for your life, then you will always face some type of opposition for that. You cannot expect everyone to be happy for you because you decide to live for Jesus.

Joseph gets thrown in a pit for his dreams and words. Getting thrown in a pit was only a stepping stone for him to get to his destiny because God intervened and had a plan and a ministry for his life. Some of you are going through turbulent situations in your life right now, you are down in a pit, and it seems like you aren't ever going to come out of your pit, but I serve notice on you that with the power of the Holy Ghost, you will come out of the pit. "I have been young, and now am old; yet have I not seen the righteous forsaken, nor his seed begging bread." (Psalm 37:25) This world is full of troubles, but there is no situation on this earth that is bigger than Jesus. Jesus can bring you out of the pit. Jesus can deliver you, and he will if you surrender to him. When someone gets arrested, they can choose to fight or surrender. It is easier when you surrender whether than to put up a fight. Some of you are in bad situations and terrible environments, but you are only in them for a season. It seemed like Joseph suffered for years, but in the middle of his suffering, God was preparing him for greatness. That is what God is doing for you; he is preparing you for greatness and he is pulling out what needs to be pulled out of you, so once you get to your destiny, you will be so humble and know that it was God that got you there. I, myself, have been through so much in life. When I was going through what I went through, it was so painful and I didn't think I was ever going to come out of it, but God brought me out. Now I am serving him with a whole and pure heart.

God had to allow Joseph to go through what he went through because it humbled him. In the end, there was a famine in the land where Jacob and his brothers lived. When it came time for Joseph and his brothers to meet, Joseph wasn't so quick to reveal himself to his brothers nor did he come out and say that Pharaoh made him in control of the whole land of Egypt. When he was with Jacob, he was quick to brag and tell his brothers what God was showing him about his future. That is why when God gives you something, you don't have to go showing and telling the whole world what God is going to do in your life because you just might run into some people like Joseph's brothers who will try to sabotage your dreams and visions from the Lord. One thing you must realize is that when you are in the pits of life, God is dealing with you and preparing you for the palace. You must know and comprehend that any and everybody can't be in the palace. The palace is for God's people. The kinds of people that will be placed in the palace are people that came from the pits of life who have given their lives over to Jesus Christ. The palace is a place of rest; it is a place where you get to enjoy what God is going to bless you with. Before you get to the palace, God has to teach you some things while you are in the pit.

Notice that before Joseph started going through the tests of life, he was quick to open his mouth to his brothers about his future.

When he went into Egypt, he wasn't quick to tell people what God was going to do through him. God has so many great things in store for you, but he can't reveal it to you until you mature in him. The enemy may be attacking you, but he cannot destroy you. It seems like when you are in the pits of life that things aren't going to work out, but God uses the pits of life to mature you and to place Godly character in you. It is God's desire for you to be saved and to be all that he has destined and called you to be. It is Jesus' desire for you to be more like him and to mature in the faith. We are living in a time and season where people don't won't to live for God. What the devil wants you to think is that you can come to God when you are ready; what a trick of the enemy. What if you die before coming to Christ? That is not what I recommend you to do because that is called gambling with your life. You only have one life to live and life is short. Living a life without Jesus Christ is very dangerous. God doesn't want you in the pit for the rest of your life. He wants to bring you out of the pits of life. He wants you out of the pit of depression. He wants you out of the pit of lying. He wants you out of the pit of abuse. He wants you out of the pit of fornication. He wants you out of the pit of excessive drinking, and drugs. The reason why I know that God wants you out of the pit is because God gave his one and only Son for us that we may be able to be redeemed from the curse of sin. "For God so loved the world, that he gave his only begotten Son." (John 3:16)

Joseph was in jail simply because Potiphar's wife wanted to commit adultery and she lied because Joseph would not lay down with her. What the woman didn't realize was that God was with Joseph; he found favor with God even when he was in jail. No matter where Joseph went, he found favor with God. Even though Joseph was in jail, he started getting exalted in jail. God is calling you into a personal relationship with him; he wants you to get to know him personally because God already knows you personally. He created you in his image and likeness. (Genesis 1:26) One of the best ways to get to know God is through renewing your mind. (Romans 12:1-2) For some of you, the very thing that may be hindering you is the way you think. You can't let the enemy control your mind; you have to have the mind of Christ. The way you start gaining the mind of Christ is by receiving the gift of salvation or getting saved. What you have to do before that is repent of your sins.

One of the things I realized about Joseph is that he had God while he was in the pit. He had God while he was in jail in Egypt because he stayed true to God in Egypt and God made him second in charge in Egypt. In a land that was foreign to him, God raised him up. I have come to realize that when you stay true to God, he will raise you up and bless you. God may not bless you when you want him to, but when he moves and when he blesses, he steps in right on time. He may not come when you want him to, but he's always right on time. When Joseph's brothers came to Egypt because of the famine and saw him, they didn't even recognize him. When Joseph saw his brothers, he wasn't so quick to say, "This is me, this is me." He was patient. Where a lot of people have messed up at is they get impatient and make decisions based on their emotions and how they feel at that time, rather than being patient, and waiting on the Lord. When you are patient and not in a hurry and you rely on God, then you will never go wrong. When Joseph didn't reveal himself to his brothers immediately, it showed and proved that he had matured in the Lord.

Once you mature in the Lord and pass the tests of life, then God will promote you. Some of you need to thank God for the stage you are in now in your life because God is trying to show you something in each stage of life that you are in. Once you learn something in each stage of life you are in, then you qualify for promotion. Elisha, for an example, was faithful to Elijah. When it was time for Elijah to go up, then because of Elisha's faithfulness, he received a double portion of the anointing of Elijah. (2Kings 2:9) As you can see, God will bless you for your obedience. That is why you should surround yourself around the right kind of people; people who love and live for God. They can help you make the right decisions. Everybody needs somebody; no one can make it without the help of another person. I must warn you that living in the fast lane of life and making a lot of bad decisions without prayer, without the Holy Spirit, and without wise Godly counsel can cripple and hinder your destiny in life and it can cause you to fall into a pit and be there for years. When you walk in righteousness, in wisdom, in patience, and in the knowledge and understanding of God's Word, you will not be consumed. What you must realize is that no matter how bad you are living, God can come in and change your whole life for the better. You will be attacked by the devil, but he cannot destroy you. You may be in the pits of life right now, but it is only going to bring out the best in you, if you will allow it to.

CHAPTER EIGHT

WHATEVER IS IN YOU WILL COME OUT OF YOU

– Matthew 15:1-20 –

Here you will find that Jesus is dealing with the Pharisees and religious leaders on God's commands and man's traditions. These Pharisees and scribes asked Jesus why his disciples broke the tradition of the elders. They asked this simply to scrutinize Jesus' activities; they were always trying to find him at fault. The Pharisees and teachers of the law came from Jerusalem, the center of Jewish authority, to downplay on Jesus. Since the Jews return from Babylonian captivity, hundreds of laws had been added to God's laws and Jesus knew that is what they were going by. They knew the law very well, but that was all they knew. The Pharisees and teachers of the law considered the laws more important rather than standing on the laws God had already established. So the Pharisees go on to say, "'Why do thy disciples transgress the tradition of the elders? For they wash not their hands when they eat bread.' But he answered and said unto them, 'Why do ye also transgress the commandment of God by your tradition?'" (Matthew 15:2-3) So here you already see that they are only trapping themselves and not Jesus. Jesus says, "For God commanded, saying, Honor thy father and mother: and, he that curseth father or mother, let him die the death." (Matthew 15:4) What Jesus was doing was exposing their hypocrisy. The Pharisees and religious leaders were hypocrites because they knew they weren't right with God, but they never wanted to acknowledge they weren't right with God. They wanted everyone to think they were so holy and right with God when they weren't right with God.

That is how a lot of so-called Christians today are; they want you to think they are so holy, but really they are just religious. That Pharisee spirit is in this 21st Century today. There are leaders in the churches today who are just simply religious. The Pharisees were religious, prideful, and full of envy, jealousy, and indignation. They were hiding their issues from the people, but not from God. He knew they were hypocrites. One thing I do realize is that you can fool man, but you cannot fool God. He knows any and everything; God knows the things that you hide in your heart. The things that you are keeping secret from man, God knows. "In the mean time, when there were gathered together an innumerable multitude of people, insomuch that they trode one upon another, he began to say unto his disciples first of all, 'Beware ye of the leaven of the Pharisees, which is hypocrisy. For there is nothing covered, that shall not be revealed; neither hid, that shall not be known. Therefore whatsoever ye have spoken in darkness shall be heard in the light; and that which ye have spoken in the ear in closets shall be proclaimed upon the housetops." (Luke 12:1-3) In other words, the Pharisees' hypocrisy would be revealed.

One thing I have realized is that what is done in the dark, or what is done when nobody is watching you, will be revealed eventually. What you have to realize is that God sees you; you may be secretly sinning where you think no one knows what you are doing, but eventually you will get caught and will be exposed for who you really are. You have to be careful as well, because you can want the respect from people and want a title for the wrong reason, and you can do crooked things to get a title. There are so many people that want titles and want degrees, but they are not willing to go through the process. There are ways now where you can buy your Doctorate degree online without ever getting your Bachelors Degree or your Masters Degree. There are also sites online where you can pay people that you don't even know and have never trained under to ordain you. They will give you a paper saying you have been ordained, but you really have not been. What that means is that you are illegally being in the pulpit and illegally having a Doctorate. You did not pay the real price to be ordained or the real price to get your Doctorate. In some denominations, you have to have a Masters of Divinity before being ordained. In my church, which is nondenominational, I had to train under my Bishop and show myself faithful to God and the church before I got ordained. I am so glad I did it God's way because now God has matured me and I see God so much clearer. I am now pursuing my Masters of Divinity. Once I get that, I will pursue my Doctor of Ministry Degree. My point is that so many people want the title so bad until they forget that God is much more concerned in you developing a relationship with him than you having a title.

There are so many people that if you don't refer to them by Pastor, Bishop, or Elder, then they will get offended; it shouldn't be like that. That is how the Pharisees were; they were so religious and stuck on titles. Anytime you will go pay someone you don't even know for ordination or for a degree, then you have missed the whole true meaning of wanting to be a leader. It is terrible what people will do today to get respect and a title. You may be able to trick man, but you cannot trick God. God is omniscient; he is all-knowing and you cannot hide anything from God. What I have discovered is that people want the titles and positions, but they don't want to go through the process to get to there. So many people try to hide things from God; it is only a trick of the enemy to think you can hide things from God. God created the universe in six days, and on the seventh day he rested. (Genesis 1 & 2) God literally spoke the cosmos, which means universe, into existence. Now if you serve a God who spoke the world into existence and he created us, then how do you think you can hide things from the divine God?

Jesus knew these religious leaders were hypocrites, but the people didn't know. The religious leaders knew Jesus knew they were hypocrites, which is one of the many reasons why they were trying to kill him and catch him into wrong. That is what some people, not all people, are seeking to do to you; they are just waiting for you to fail, but God wants you to keep your head. Know that he is on your side. I don't care if you were raised in the projects. I don't care if your dad never showed you he loved you. I don't care if your parents hate each other or got a divorce. I don't care if you grew up poor. If you stand on God's Holy Word and keep God first, watch him do the miraculous in your life. I don't care if people said you would never make it, you show them and the devil that you can and will make it. The best way to defeat the devil and your enemies is to be successful. Another way to defeat your enemies is to be successful in Christ Jesus, and your life will never be the same. There were so many people that thought I wouldn't make it, but look at what God has done; look at what God is doing in my life. This is one of the many books I will be writing unto the Lord and for God's people. It was prophesied to me that I would be writing books, and now I am doing it with the help of the Holy Spirit. I really sought the Lord on what to write on, and about, and he wanted me to start out in this book talking about my life, and then go into spiritual truths.

Jesus says, "But ye say, Whosoever shall say to his father or his mother, It is a gift, by whatsoever thou mightest be profited by me; And honor not his father or his mother, he shall be free. Thus have ye made the commandment of God of none effect by your tradition." (Matthew 15:5-6) This practice was the practice of Corban, which literally means offering. Anyone who made a Corban vow, was required to dedicate money to God's temple, which otherwise would have gone to support their parents. Corban had become a religiously acceptable way to neglect parents. These religious leaders were ignoring God's clear command to honor their parents.

We are living in a time today in this 21st Century, where people and kids don't want to honor and respect their parents. Now I am not saying you have to agree with your parents when they are wrong, because as a believer you have to stand on God's Word and what is right in God's eyes. Young people today think they know more than their parents, not knowing that their parents want the best for them, and they don't want them to make the same mistakes they have made in the past. Jesus says, "Ye hypocrites, well did Isaiah prophesy of you, saying, This people draweth nigh unto me with their mouth, and honoreth me with their lips; but their heart is far from me. But in vain they do worship me, teaching for doctrines the commandments of men." (Matthew 15:7-9) I must state, there are so many people proclaiming Christianity, but their walk and things they have in their heart make you wonder if they really are who they serve, which is Christ. I understand and know that no one is perfect; I know that someone can want to do right and have a heart to really serve God, but they are caught up in their flesh and addictions. However, when you don't want to do right and know what is right, then that is a major problem. In the past, I had problems and had the heart of God and wanted to do right, but got caught up in my addiction, and fell short. I thank God for deliverance because now I am not the same and I will never be the same again in my life. I can honestly say if I were to die now, I would go to heaven. That is the kind of assurance I have about myself. Am I perfect? No! Do I fall short at times? Yes! Will I go to heaven? Yes! There are so many people today that don't want to admit they have issues and then they judge the other believers who are struggling in order to take the focus off of their baggage.

Just like the religious leaders: they were hypocrites, they were traditional, and they used their traditions and laws for the wrong reasons. They abused the power that they had. That is what so many believers do today. They abuse their power and they spiritually abuse God's people. God is looking for people who are going to be sincere with him and with other people. I will tell you that I make mistakes and I have struggled in my flesh a lot of times, even while being saved. It is a shame that so many Christians try to be someone they really are not. One of the problems that I noticed about the Pharisees is that they were easily to get angered. When Jesus was around and when Jesus taught and did miracles, they were angry and full of indignation.

As a leader, you should be slow to anger. So many times, satan gets so-called believers angry easily. I have realized that when you are easily to get angry, then that tells a lot about who you are and your character as well. If you are a Pastor, Bishop, teacher, preacher, or Evangelist, you must be slow to anger. If people see you are easily to get offended and upset, then the babes in Christ will think it is okay and the mature believers will know it is a problem. In Luke 13, Jesus healed a woman that was crippled for 18 years and she glorified God. The synagogue ruler was filled with indignation, meaning he got jealous and was easily angered over what Jesus had done for this woman. He may have felt that way because of how the people responded to what Jesus had done, and all the attention was off of him and on Jesus. My take on this is that when souls are getting saved, delivered, set free, and walking into their destiny, it doesn't have to be me that is be the one God is using. As long as souls get saved and people get healed and delivered, then I am happy. The religious leaders had no integrity, no character and they were morally corrupt. They were clean on the outside, but they were filthy on the inside. Jesus called the crowd to him and said, "Not that which goeth into the mouth defileth a man; but that which cometh out of the mouth, this defileth a man." (Matthew 15:11)

Whatever is in you, will come out of you and that is fact. If jealousy is in you, then it is jealousy that will come out of you. Now let me state, this book isn't to judge you or come down on you, this book is to reveal the truth to you so you can be a better believer; for the unbelievers to see that satan is the one that has you bound. This book is to take the fish scales off of your eyes. This book is designed for you to know the truth and see the truth; to make you see that you need to make a change for the better and accept Jesus as your Lord and Savior, so he can take away all of the bad habits that you possess. I love everyone that is reading this book. So many ministers aren't giving the truth, but I am a young Pastor that stands on the truth. The truth hurts a lot of times, but it will save you in the end. In this world today, people don't want to know the truth and they would rather live on false hope; they'd rather live in and walk in the flesh, than walk in the spirit. To walk in the spirit means you have to let go of the fleshly things of this world. I must tell the truth because I am on a mission for Jesus. One day I will stand before him and I want him to say, "Tommy, well done, thou good and faithful servant." (Matthew 25:21) At the end of my ministry, I want to say like Paul said, "I have fought a good fight, I have finished my course, I have kept the faith." (2Timothy 4:7) This is my heart and this is the kind of preacher and Pastor I am. I have to tell the truth, even if it hurts you because I love you and in the end it will help you and benefit you.

If hatred is in you, then that is what will proceed out of you. If unforgiveness is in you, then it is going to come out of you. If low self-esteem is in you, then that is what will come out of you. If doubt and fear are in you, then they will proceed out of you. Whatever is in you, will come out of you. If love is in you, then love will come out of you. If joy is in you, then joy will come out of you. If peace is in you, then peace will come out of you. If faith is in you, then faith is what will come out of you. If gentleness is in you, then gentleness will come out of you. So again, whatever is in you is what will proceed out of you. Have you ever heard someone say something real bad and then say, "Well, I didn't mean to say that."? That was in their heart in the beginning. The truth of the matter is, that may not be who you are, but it is in you. If you are honest and acknowledge it is in you, then God can take it out of you. What I have discovered is that a lot of Christians can't get free from things that are in them because of pride. They won't admit that they have issues and problems and that they really need Jesus to deliver them. That is how God delivered me; I was truthful and I was honest with God and I was honest with myself. So many Christians want to try and convince other people that they have arrived, but the truth is they have not arrived. One of the best ways you can witness to this lost world is for a believer to admit that they still have issues and still has missed the mark. God is calling his people to be clean on the inside. If you are clean on the inside, then other people will begin to see the light in you. If other people cannot correct you without you getting offended, then you might have the spirit of a Pharisee.

When Jesus would correct the Pharisees, then they would get so easily upset and angry because they knew he was right and they were wrong. Being that they were so full of pride, they didn't want to be corrected. They were full of jealousy and tried to kill Jesus all because of the truth. What God is looking for is for some people in this 21st Century that are going to stand on the truth. I must say that standing on the truth is not a popular thing to do because so many people want to live by and walk in the spirit of deception. It is a sacrifice to walk in the truth, but the reward is great. "To obey is better than sacrifice." (1Samuel 15:22) God showed me that sometimes it takes a sacrifice to be obedient. What God showed me is that the Word of God is the truth. So many people want to go to churches where their emotions are being tickled and where there is no kind of Word being preached to them that can change their lives for the better. They go in the church a devil, and come out of the church a devil. I told God that if I never have a big church, I will always preach the Word of God and preach the truth in love.

The disciples came to Jesus and asked, "Knowest thou that the Pharisees were offended, after they heard this saying? But he answered and said, 'Every plant, which my heavenly Father hath not planted, shall be rooted up. Let them alone: they be blind leaders of the blind. And if the blind lead the blind, both shall fall into the ditch.'" (Matthew 15:12-14) In other words, Jesus was saying to leave the Pharisees alone because the Pharisees were blind to God's truth. Anyone who would listen to their teachings would risk going spiritually blind as well. That is why it is important that you sit under a ministry where you are hearing the truth being preached, even if it hurts, it is still the truth. "For the word of God is quick, and powerful, and sharper than any two-edged sword, piercing even to the dividing asunder of soul and spirit, and of the joints and marrow, and is a discerner of the thoughts and intents of the heart. Neither is there any creature that is not manifest in his sight: but all things are naked and opened unto the eyes of him with whom we have to do." (Hebrews 4:12-13) In other words, the word of God is simply a collection of words from God; it's living, it's life changing, and like when a surgeon has his knife for surgery, the Word of God reveals who we are and who we are not; it penetrates to our moral and spiritual being and it discerns what is in us, both good and evil. Once you hear the Word of God, you have to make a decision to accept it or to reject it. There are consequences for both decisions. You must not just listen and hear the Word of God, but you must also allow it to change your life and shape you into who God has called you to be. "But be ye doers of the word, and not hearers only, deceiving your own selves." (James 1:22)

These Pharisees were claiming that they knew the God of Israel; they claimed to know the God of Abraham, Isaac, and Jacob, but they really didn't know God. If they would have known God, then they would have known that Jesus is the Messiah, the Christ, the Anointed One, and the Son of the Living God. If you don't believe that Jesus is these names that I have said, then it is impossible to make it into heaven. It is sad to say that today in the 21st Century churches, you have Pharisee Pastors and preachers in the pulpit; they have no character, no integrity, no power, and no fruit of the Holy Spirit; they are acting like somebody they aren't; they only possess titles. There are Pharisee leaders and members in the churches of today.

The way Jesus deals with them is he walks in truth right in front of them. No matter how they act, Jesus still remains faithful to his calling and to his people. That is what believers have to do; stand on the truth and stand on the Word of God in any situation. When you see people leaving God and the church, then you should still stay and remain in God, no matter what you see. You can't let what you see in the church cause you to fall away from God. No matter what happens to you, no matter what the devil throws your way, you have to do like Jesus did and stand on the Word of God. You need to keep your Godly character, keep your integrity and be obedient to God regardless of what goes on around you. The question is: can you remain obedient to God when everyone has turned their back on God? Can you remain obedient to God under pressure? God is calling you to be a leader and not a follower. It isn't popular to be a Christian and it isn't popular to walk in obedience, but there is a great reward in the end for remaining true to God. Can you serve God even though everyone else is falling into the traps of the devil? Can you serve God and stay on the path to heaven when your closest friends, family, and loved ones have turned their backs on God? Will you still continue to stand? Can you still stand strong in the Lord when you know that you have loved ones, friends, and family members who are hypocrites?

I must state these issues because it is reality. What I have realized as a young Pastor is that people don't want to deal with and face reality. Reality is something you must deal with and face. For an example, the reality is that someday we have to die and leave this earth. Now that is reality, whether we want to face it or not, we will face it one day. As much as people love this world, we must one day leave it behind. We will have to let everything in this world go and leave it behind one day. The nice cars, all of the money, our spouses, children, family, friends, jobs, loved ones, houses, and businesses; we will all die and leave all of it behind us one day. There are two appointments we must spiritually face one day: death and being judged by God on the judgment day after we die. Those are two things that we cannot get around. There are two things I know he may tell you: "Welcome into heaven." or "Depart from me." and you will be cast into the Lake of fire, which is another term for Hell. Can you stand and walk in holiness, even when some of the most respected leaders have fallen?

Jesus says, "Whatsoever entereth in at the mouth goeth into the belly, and is cast out into the draught." (Matthew 15:17) Jesus is using a biological example to get a spiritual truth across to his people. Jesus says, "No man putteth new wine into old bottles; else the new wine will burst the bottles, and be spilled, and the bottles shall perish. But new wine must be put into new bottles; and both are preserved." (Luke 5:37-38) Jesus was talking about wineskins, which were goatskins sewn together at the edges to form watertight bags. New wine expands as it ages; it has to be put into new wineskins. An old wineskin would burst and spill the wine. Like old wineskins, the Pharisees were too religious and hypocritical to accept Jesus. Jesus could not be contained in the traditions or rules that they made up. As true believers, we represent the new wine; the old bottle is the old you, the fleshy you. If you try to take the new you into the old you, then it will contaminate the new you. That is why you who are the new wine must stay in the new bottle, so you won't burst and act out in the flesh. That is why you need the new bottle, which is Jesus Christ, so you won't burst that which is the new you. New wine, new you; new wine, new bottle. The new wine and new bottle represent the new you, the holy you, the sanctified you, the Holy Ghost filled you, the slow to get mad you, the fruit of the Spirit you, the person with integrity and Godly character you. The flesh cannot agree with the Spirit, so God is calling you to be of the Spirit and not of your flesh. Acting out in your flesh has gotten you nowhere, so why not try the Holy Spirit. When you are always operating in your flesh, then that will cause you to make bad and fleshly decisions, simply because of your negative mindset.

Jesus says, "But those things which proceed out of the mouth come forth from the heart; and they defile the man. For out of the heart proceed evil thoughts, murders, adulteries, fornications, thefts, false witness, blasphemies: These are the things which defile a man: but to eat with unwashen hands defileth not a man." (Matthew 15:18-20) So many men and women work hard to keep themselves looking good on the outside, but what about the heart? Do you take as much time to make sure you are right on the inside as you do your outside? Some people love to work out every day at the gym; there is nothing wrong with that, but we must work out spiritually as well. You should bench press the Word of God daily so you can be a better Christian or become a believer. Run on the treadmill of the scriptures. Do some abs work of prayer. Run laps of righteousness. Lift the weights of the sword of the Spirit, which is the Word of God. When you are tested and tried, then nothing but righteousness will proceed out of your heart.

CHAPTER NINE

THE CHAINS IN YOUR LIFE ARE LOOSE

– Acts 16:22-35 –

It may seem like nothing in your life is going right for you and all odds are against you, but what you have to realize is that "all things work together for good." (Romans 8:28) What you must realize and comprehend is that everything happens for a reason and God allows so many things to happen in our lives for a reason. In this world there is a reason for everything; every decision an individual makes, whether for the good or for the bad, they do it for a reason. God will allow you to make your own decisions in life, but when you are ready to surrender your life to him, he is ready to take you on. In the book of Acts, Paul and Silas were both imprisoned for doing the will of God. They were going to pray and everyone in the public knew they were going to pray; they were on their way to pray and there was a slave girl who had a spirit by which she could predict the future. (Acts 16:16) She earned a lot of money for her owners; satan presents himself as an angel of light. (2Corinthians 11:14) In other words, satan and his servants can deceive us by appearing to be attractive, good, and moral. Don't be fooled by outside appearances because our impressions alone are not an accurate indicator of who is or isn't a true follower of Christ. You must ask yourself, does what this leader teaches line up with scripture? (Acts 17:11) Does this leader believe and preach that Jesus Christ is the Son of the Living God who came into this world as a man to save us from sins? (1John 4:1-3) Is this teacher's lifestyle consistent with the Word of God? (Matthew 12:33-37) You must understand that satan has his demonic hosts assigned to your life to try and get you away from God and cause you to not come into relationship with Jesus Christ. As long as you stick with Jesus Christ and stay under his blood, then you will be covered by the blood of Jesus Christ. I know it may seem like things aren't getting better and it may seem like the more you try to serve God, then the more bad things start happening, but that is only a test to see if you will remain with God when things don't look so good. Anyone can serve God when everything is always going their way. Can you serve God even while everything isn't going your way? When the storms of life come your way, can you stay true to God? When you stand true to God while you are experiencing bad things, then sooner or later, the good days will come. "What shall we then say to these things? If God be for us, who can be against us?" (Romans 8:31) God loves us unconditionally. The reason why I know he loves us is because he gave his one and only Son Jesus, who was perfect and innocent as a lamb, to take away the sins of the world. What satan wants to do is make you think God isn't there for you just because life's situations seem to bring you down. The truth of the matter is that God is always with you because God is everywhere.

This slave girl followed Paul and the rest of them shouting that, "These men are the servants of the most high God, which show unto us the way of salvation." (Acts 16:17) So it is obvious that this spirit knew what Paul's mission was and who he stood for; that spirit or demon recognized the God in Paul and his followers. She kept this up many days and Paul became troubled. He turned around and spoke to the spirit. Now notice he spoke to the spirit, meaning he spoke directly to the demon. Notice what the demon said through the slave girl. What it said through this slave girl was true, but it was the source in which it came from. This true statement was made from an evil force, so therefore it could not be received. If Paul would have received this statement the demon said when it said, "You are servants of the Most High God." then that would mean Paul was somewhat agreeing with demonic activity; that was something Paul definitely wasn't going to. He spoke directly to the spirit in this young slave girl. Paul spoke to the spirit and not the woman and said, "I command thee in the name of Jesus Christ to come out of her." (Acts 16:18) God wants us to use his Son Jesus' name against satan's fallen angels. Notice now, Paul didn't say "I, Paul, command you to come out of her," but he said in the name of Jesus Christ I command you to come out of her.

Some things happen for the better when you use the name of Jesus. Demons tremble at the name of Jesus Christ. Why did he say this in the name of Jesus? He said this in the name of Jesus simply because he understood the power and authority that Jesus Christ has over satan and his demons. There is power in the name of Jesus. Paul was anointed by God to do ministry and cast out demons. He used the name of Jesus against the powers of satan. As a believer, you have to use the name of Jesus Christ and plead his blood over any situation you find yourself in. You can't always depend on a minister because you won't always be around them. When the devil comes against you and attacks you, then you have to call on the name of Jesus for yourself, rebuke the devil yourself, and speak to the devil using the name of Jesus. The name of Jesus Christ doesn't just work for pastors or ordained ministers; it works for every believer who calls on his name with a pure and sincere heart. You must comprehend that the enemy only has power when you give it to him. He does not possess the omnipotent power that God has; God is all powerful. It may seem like things aren't working out for you. It may seem like the situation is getting worse, but you have to keep calling on the name of Jesus Christ. The more you call on Jesus, the stronger you will become spiritually and the stronger your faith will become. God is on your side even when you don't think he is. I know it seems like you can't feel God or sense his presence, but you can't go by feelings when it comes to God. "For we walk by faith, not by sight." (2Corinthians 5:7)

At that moment, the spirit left the slave girl and she could no longer do the duty of fortune telling anymore. She could no longer make her owners any more money and they got upset and reported Paul and Silas to the authorities. They dragged them in for them to be punished and persecuted. I have come to the conclusion that sometimes you have to go through certain things in life to appreciate what God has for you. For example, in Genesis 37, Joseph would always tell his brothers what God revealed to him in his dreams. I am not saying that Joseph didn't appreciate his gifts, but God took him through some things that matured him into his destiny. Sometimes God has to mature you into your destiny so you won't abort your destiny. If everything was given to you so easily, then you probably wouldn't appreciate God's blessings. What God has to do is allow you to go through some things so it can mature you in your faith and so you can handle what he wants to bless you with. The city was in an uproar because of what happened. The problem was that they were Christians and the Romans could not accept that. One of the many reasons I believe it is hard for people to give their lives to Jesus Christ is because they are afraid of what other people will think of them. They think they will lose out on a lot and lose out on friends. I believe if your friends walk out on you because you gave your life to Jesus Christ so you could miss hell, then the truth of the matter is they were not your friends in the beginning. A true friend will tell you that you need to give your life to Jesus Christ.

"And the multitude rose up together against them: and the magistrates rent off their clothes, and commanded to beat them." (Acts 16:22) They were stripped and beaten all because of the Gospel of Jesus Christ. The Gospel is simply the Good News. You must comprehend that when you make it up in your mind that you are going to live for Jesus Christ, you can look for the devil to get an attitude with you and attack you violently. Many people don't want to be Christians simply because of what people will say about them. They are afraid of how people will view them if they are a Christian. I must say to the nonbelievers, don't let what people say about you or Christians make you miss out on heaven. You cannot have your cake and eat it too. In order to make it into heaven, you must make a sacrifice. Jesus says, "For whosoever shall be ashamed of me and of my words, of him shall the Son of man be ashamed, when he shall come in his own glory, and in his Father's, and of the holy angels." (Luke 9:26) Paul and Silas were two men who still held on to their faith in Jesus Christ in spite of all the persecution they went through. That lets us know that we can hold on too; no matter what the enemy throws our way. They were thrown into prison. Not only were they thrown into prison, but they were put into the worst part, which was called a dungeon, with other prisoners. Chains were put on their feet, along with all the bruises from them getting beaten. A jailer was commanded to guard them carefully.

The revelation to this is that no matter how bound a true believer may be God has a way of taking the shackles off their feet. Some of you may be in a dungeon based on what you are going through in this life. You have had chains on you for so long and you don't know what it is like to be free. The chains in your life are about to fall off. The devil should have taken you out when he had the chance, but it is too late now. You have come too far to give up now. I don't care how bad your life is; the enemy will try to throw any and everything your way to keep the chains on your feet. When you find your back is up against the wall, just begin to develop a life of prayer. Even if you don't know how to pray, just call on the name of Jesus until you learn how to pray. Just learn the name of Jesus and realize the power alone in that name. They were in jail and at about midnight and Paul and Silas began to pray and praise God while locked up in a dungeon. The revelation to this that God gave me is that Paul and Silas were innocent and did no wrong, but did something for God and for this slave girl. Even in them being locked up, they still had joy. Even though they had chains on their feet, were locked up, and had been beaten severely, they still had peace. Out of them being beaten up and locked up, God still worked it out for the good. The jailer and his whole household were saved out of Paul and Silas's severe persecution.

What you must realize is that God will get the glory out of what you are going through. If you will allow him, he will reveal himself to you in the middle of your storm, in due time. Paul and Silas were singing hymns to God and they were so loud that the other prisoners were listening to them. (Acts 16:25) No matter where they were, they still made the best of it. They did not let the kind of environment they were in change them, but they changed the environment they were in for the better. That is what the problem is with people today; they say it is hard to be a Christian and the people they associate with aren't Christians; that is nothing but an excuse. If you really want to change, you will change. When you really want to live for Jesus, then he will make a way for you to change your life for the better. When Paul and Silas started to pray, something happened. "And suddenly there was a great earthquake, so that the foundations of the prison were shaken." (Acts 16:26) That is one thing God will do when his people get caught up in bad situations; he will shake the foundations of trials and tribulations for his people. God is always on your side and he expects you to put your faith and trust in him in the most horrendous type of situations. It may be an attack on your family, marriage, ministry, pastor, finances, or body, but just keep praying like Paul and Silas and know that eventually, the chains on your life will be loosed.

Paul and Silas's and everyone's chains fell off in the prison. The revelation to that is that there were people that were in prison with them and their chains fell off too; because Paul and Silas had a direct relationship with Jesus and they prayed all night, God moved on their behalf. They never lost hope and they kept the faith in the middle of a terrible situation; because of that, lives were changed.

When the jailer woke up and saw all the prison doors open, he automatically got ready to kill himself with the sword. Paul said to him, "Do yourself no harm: for we are all here." (Acts 16:28) If you are on the verge of suicide, please don't harm yourself. Jesus Christ is the answer to your problem. The jailer trembled with fear and asked Paul and Silas, "Sirs, what must I do to be saved?" They replied, "Believe on the Lord Jesus Christ, and thou shalt be saved, and thy house." (Acts 16:30-31) That is why you must believe that the chains in your life are loose! It doesn't matter what you are going through, the chains are loose in your life. Give God the glory because the chains are loose in your life! If you are not saved, I ask you to make him your Lord and Savior today, so the chains on your life will be loosed and you will be qualified for eternal life.

CHAPTER TEN

GOD IS CALLING YOUR NAME

– Luke 5:1-11 –

Jesus provides a miraculous catch of fish and he also calls his disciples to follow him. I theologically believe that Jesus did this miracle for these fishermen not just to help them, but for them to see who he was and what he was about to ask them to do. The people crowded around him and listened to the Word of God as he stood by Lake Gennesaret. These people literally pressed to get near him. The Greek word for 'pressed' means imposed or forced. It could have been that they were not necessarily going to hear the Word, but they could have been going just to impose or see who this Jesus was. He carried himself so differently and taught a doctrine that was so different from the other teachings they had been getting. Jesus had been teaching and preaching in the synagogues and had been casting out unclean spirits. It could have been for a number of reasons why they were coming to hear Jesus. What Jesus did was he took advantage of their curiosity and he used it wisely. What is your main purpose for coming going to church? Perhaps you don't go to church. If you don't go to church, you must understand that you need a covering. Church is a place where you learn about God and you learn the things of God. Your purpose for going to church should be to develop a relationship with Jesus Christ.

Jesus systematically questioned this disciple concerning taking the ship out a little from the land. Not only was Jesus concerned about preaching to these people, but he was concerned about who he would choose to be his disciples. Jesus knew that he was fully human and not just fully God alone, so he knew he would need help in the ministry that he was about to do on this earth. God was simply calling their names. The Bible says that Jesus sat down and taught the people out of the ship. No matter where Jesus was, he made the best out of it. Every opportunity he got to preach and teach the Word of God, he took advantage of that. That is how believers should be when it comes to sinners or people who are not saved; every chance you as a believer get, you should share Jesus Christ with people. Being that Jesus was fully human meant that he could not be everywhere present at the same time. He was incarnate, meaning he had a bodily form. He called out his disciples for help so he could go forth into ministry, and he later ordained them as Apostles. You must understand that as a believer, nobody can do it all by themselves. If Jesus Christ needed help, then we also will need help. God is calling us to be accountable. So many people today don't want to be accountable to anyone; but the disciples were accountable to Jesus and in the end it blessed their earthly ministry and they were so effective in their ministry. One thing I realize about accountability is that when you are accountable to another strong believer, then that will keep you out of a lot of sin. That person that is holding you responsible is there to keep you on the right track. For example, let's say you want to stop doing a particular sin that you know is wrong and you tell one of your close friends to make sure that you don't continue in this sin; that is a form of accountability and that is something every person that is seeking deliverance should have is an accountability partner. The truth is that more people in the church need to be accountable. That would keep them out of a lot of trouble if they were accountable to an individual who is strong in the faith.

When Jesus had finished speaking, he said to Simon, "Launch out into the deep, and let down your nets for a draught." (Luke 5:4) Jesus just finishes another one of his powerful messages and now he is starting to deal with his future disciples and his future Apostles.

That is what God is doing for you who are reading this book; Jesus is calling your name because he loves you and he died for your sins. He wants you to step out on faith and know that he is God and that he can change your life. If he has already changed your life, he wants you to draw closer to him. Jesus wants you to pray more, read his Word more, spend more time with him and share the Gospel of Jesus Christ to the people he has called you to. Everyone has a ministry. I am not saying everyone is called to preach, but God has a person or people that he has called you to reach. We are all called to witness the Gospel to his people.

As God is beginning to deal with his chosen people by this miraculous catch of fish, God showed me that he can meet you anywhere you want him to. God can meet you on a cruise. God can meet you in the middle of your sin. God can meet you in jail. God can meet you in the middle of any bad situation you are enduring. God is calling your name. God is calling you out of the bondage of sin; God is calling you out of that sinful lifestyle you have been in for years. You may think that if you go to church then that is good enough. Yes, it is good to go to church; but once you get in church, you must allow the Holy Spirit to change you for the better. Church alone cannot save you. In order for you to be saved, you must first repent of your sins and turn from your wicked ways. Then you must accept the gift of salvation or get saved by accepting Jesus Christ as your personal Lord and Savior. (Romans 10:9) This thing has to be personal; he wants to personally have a relationship with you. God wants you to take time out of your busy schedule to spend time with him so you can grow in the knowledge of God.

Jesus tells Simon to launch out into the deep; that is what God is calling you to do is to launch out into the deep for whatever it is that you are believing God for. The Greek for launch means to put out. If you want anything from God, if you want more of God, you have to be willing to put down anything that isn't like God. God is calling your name. God is calling you into obedience to his Word. God is calling you to be more like him. God is calling you to give your whole entire life to him. Why not trust God with your life? You have trusted satan with your life for so many years and it has gotten you nowhere at all. Think about all the decisions you made without God; look where it has gotten you. What you must realize is that you were bought with a price. (1Corithians 7:23) Your life doesn't belong to you, but it belongs to God. The sooner you realize that, the better off you will be. Take time out and ask yourself, if you would have prayed before making certain decisions and been patient and waited on the Holy Spirit, would you be in as much trouble as you are in or have been in? Many of you have been divorced simply because you didn't pray before going into holy matrimony. You always have to have an attitude of prayer. When you have an attitude of prayer, it will keep you out of a lot of things. Many people get hurt in life simply because they don't pray before doing things. You must put your total trust in God and not man. Man will let you down, but God will never fail you. Is the weight of the sins of this world worth you not launching out into the deep to get what God has for you? What I mean by launching out into the deep for God is getting to know God to the point that you will no longer want sin to be a part of your life; until that addiction will no longer have a stronghold on you. "For the wages of sin is death; but the gift of God is eternal life through Jesus Christ our Lord." (Romans 6:23) If you sow into sin, then sin is what you will reap. If you sow into righteousness, then righteousness is what you will reap. What God wants you to do is launch your net out into righteousness and not darkness. He wants you to launch out into understanding and come into the knowledge of who he is.

These disciples Jesus chose, they didn't understand and know who Jesus really was in the beginning. These were ordinary men, destined and chosen for greatness. That is what God will do; he will choose ordinary people that don't seem like they have a future and God will choose them and raise them up and use them mightily. Moses had a speech problem, but God still used him mightily to deliver the Israelites out of Egypt. Jeremiah said, "Lord God! behold, I cannot speak: for I am a child." (Jeremiah 1:6-7) God still used him mightily. God chose a man named Abraham and made him the father of many nations. God saw these sinners who Jesus called to be disciples for who they would be in the ending and did not go by the beginning of who they were. So many of you have issues with loved ones, family members, or children and you think that they will never change. God will never give up on them and you should keep the faith that God can change them. God is a God who can make the impossible possible. That is how it is for you; God is telling you to launch out into the deep seas of life, come to him and let him show you the finished you. Every person who is reading this book is destined for greatness. It may seem like satan is throwing so much opposition your way to confuse you of who you are to become in God. You as a believer must keep the faith and not go by what you see with your natural eye, but go by what you see with your spiritual eyes. Close your eyes and use the weapon of faith. When you close our eyes to use the weapon of faith, then faith can take you where your natural eyes can't. Faith can get you healed even when you are sick. Faith can bring financial freedom when you are broke. Faith can get your family saved when they are acting like the devil. Faith can get you a house when you are staying in an apartment. Faith can get you transportation when you are always taking the bus. Faith can get you delivered from sin when you are in bondage to sin.

I am telling you today, God is calling your name. God is calling you to seek his face and God is calling you to draw closer to him and to rely upon his strength and not your own. Satan wants you to focus on the negative mistakes you have made so you won't be able to see yourself as God sees you. God sees you healed. God sees you delivered from addictions. God sees you set free. God even sees you mentoring other disciples in the kingdom of God. Satan does not want you to see yourself how God sees you because if you ever see yourself how God sees you in the future, you will be a threat to his kingdom. God wants you to know that he is calling you by your name and he is calling you to launch out into the deep and find out who you really are in him. God told them to let down their nets for a draught, meaning in the Greek a haul or a catching of the fish. Jesus could have been demonstrating this to let them know the authority he has even over nature. These disciples had already heard of him because they were obedient to what Jesus had told them to do and they were blessed by it.

One thing you must realize and understand is that when you are obedient to God and his Word, you can look to be blessed by God. If so many people in the church would be patient and do what the

Word of God says, then imagine how powerful the church would be today. God is calling for his people to unite with each other and come together, but it seems like today in this 21st Century that churches are so divided. Preachers are jealous of other preachers, members are jealous of other members, and people in the church are jealous of other people's positions in the body of Christ. The reality is that all positions in the church are important because we are the body of Christ. It seems like the church is somewhat losing its witness because of how believers are conducting themselves. God is coming back for his church and he is coming back for the body of Christ. Simon said, "Master, we have toiled all the night," meaning they tried all night long to catch fish and they were not successful at all until the Master showed up. (Luke 5:5)

Many of you have toiled so long for the world and for the devil and you have toiled for years in the flesh. Now God is calling you to toil in the spirit. You have toiled for years for addictions and now God is calling your name and making you to toil after the lost souls. This is a lost and dying world and people that are in this world are spiritually dead and they don't even know it. The people that are bound by their sins think that what they are doing is right. One thing I have realized is that satan has a major hold on the young people. I was a mentor and a group leader for the schools and sometimes a conversation about God would come up because they knew I was a preacher. They knew I was a preacher and they still had no respect and they were very rebellious. What God showed me was that it was how they are being raised at home and their surroundings. Kids would say things like you don't have to love people to go to heaven; you can go to heaven without Jesus; you can do this and that and still go to heaven. What you have to realize is that they were taught that doctrine from somewhere. One of the main things of the Doctrine of Jesus Christ is love. It is impossible to go to heaven without walking in love. You cannot walk in unforgiveness and live any kind of lifestyle and then think you are going to heaven; it doesn't work that way.

It is amazing that Simon here refers to Jesus as 'master', but later on refers to him as the Son of the Living God. You must know and understand that it takes revelation from God and the Holy Ghost for you to realize who Jesus is. He is more than just a Rabbi (which means teacher); he is more than Master; he is more than just a prophet; he is the Prince of Peace, the Almighty God, the Messiah, Christ the Anointed One, and the Son of the Living God. The only way you can get to God is through Jesus. Jesus is the one and only true God. My question to you is what is Jesus to you? Is he just a rabbi, is he just Master, or is he your Lord and Savior? If you are reading this book and you happen to not be saved, I must be honest and tell you the only way to heaven is through Jesus Christ. You must confess and believe that he is the Son of the Living God in order to be saved and go to heaven. (Romans 10:9) Is Jesus just someone you call on when you get in trouble or need a serious breakthrough? Can you launch out and grab a hold of him in the sea of your situation? Simon may have referred to him as Master because at that time, he had no revelation that Jesus was the Savior of man. For some people, it is going to take some kind of experience for them to realize who Jesus is to them and to this world.

I tell you boldly, whether you want to believe it or not, that Jesus Christ is the Messiah and he is the Son of the Living God. A person that doesn't believe that doesn't take away his power or authority; it just means that that person who doesn't believe is spiritually blind and is on their way to destruction. Jesus is the Almighty God who is in control of everything; he is in control of people's destinies and he is in control of people's purposes. Some people who died and got killed before walking into their purpose; God still had a plan and a purpose for their life. You must know and understand that God is calling your name and he does have a plan for your life. God knows you better than you know yourself. You must know that God is in total control of humanity and you don't know yourself like God knows you. That is why it is important that you trust him with your life. He knows where he wants you to be and who he wants you to be with. Many people have gotten involved with people that turned out to be sent from the devil. They were so into that person and they didn't think that person would hurt them, but now that person has become their worst nightmare. That is why it is important that when people want to inquire of you, you must be prayerful about it. They could be an enemy in disguise. It takes revelation and revelatory experience for you to realize who Christ is. Revelation is an act of revealing or astonishment or excitement in knowing of something that you never knew of before. Now that you have been through some things, you now see and know that Jesus is real.

Simon says, "Nevertheless at thy word I will let down the net." (Luke 5:5) In other words, he says that since the Master has spoken and I have heard this awesome preaching and the miracles Jesus has done then I am going to obey him. When you let go of the things of the flesh for the sake of Jesus Christ, then you are setting yourself up for eternal heaven. When you let go of the world and bondage for Jesus Christ, then you are setting yourself up to be blessed. Be careful though, because your purpose for serving God shouldn't be just to be blessed; your purpose for serving him should be because he is God, because he is worthy, because he first loved you and then because of that, he will bless you. So many people try to come to God for the wrong reasons, thinking if they let go of this, then God will do this or give them this amount of money or whatever the case may be; that isn't how it works. What if God doesn't give you that promotion, then will you serve him? What if you don't get approved for the house when you want it to happen, will you still serve him? What if you don't get the car you want, will you still serve him and believe that he is still a prayer answering God? You must know that God is still a prayer answering God even if he doesn't answer your prayers the way you want him to. You must know and understand that you don't control God, but God controls you. He has your life already mapped out and he is going to answer prayers according to his will because he knows what is best for you. So why don't you just surrender and give up the things of this world to follow a God who will never let you down? When you renew your mind with the Word of God, it broadens your ability to see things in a whole different perspective for the better. For example, now that you know that drinking excessive wine and drinking alcohol is sin and that it is destroying you physically and spiritually and having sex out of marriage and being on drugs is also sin and that it can also destroy you physically and spiritually, you won't ever be the same.

(1Corinthians 6:12-20, 1Timothy 3:8) "And be not drunk with wine, wherein is excess; but be filled with the Spirit." (Ephesians 5:18)

Simon responded out of obedience; even though he didn't know God, it caused him to get what he had been trying to get all night long. As you begin to be obedient to God, it will cause you to receive what God has for you. My point is that even if you are not familiar with Jesus in the beginning of your walk with Jesus, if you respond in faith and let go of the sins of this world, then you will gain so much more physically, spiritually and emotionally.

"They enclosed a great multitude of fishes; and their net broke." (Luke 5:6) In other words, they received so many fish until what they had could not even contain the blessing that Jesus gave them. They received this blessing simply out of obedience. You must know and understand that being obedient to God will cause you to be blessed. Just because Abraham was obedient to God and he stepped out not knowing where he was going, God made him the father of many nations. Today we are Abraham's seed, simply out of his obedience. (Genesis 12) They really didn't know who Jesus was, but they were still obedient. When you are obedient to the Word of God, eventually, when it is your time and season, God will bless you. What I have discovered is that people want God to move according to their timing; but God doesn't move how we move, he moves according to how he wants to move. That is something you cannot and will not change about God. God has no one to answer to but himself. He is only responsible to himself. God existed before the foundations of the earth. If God has not given you what you have been asking him for yet, there is a reason why he has not given it to you. He knows something you don't know.

God was preparing these disciples to be fishermen of men. God was calling their names and God was calling their faithfulness to discipleship. This was their last catch of fish because God was going to make these disciples fishermen of men and not fish. "And they beckoned unto their partners, which were in the other ship, that they should come and help them. And they came, and filled both the ships, so that they began to sink." (Luke 5:7) In other words, they had so much fish and so much of a blessing that they needed help. "When Simon Peter saw it, he fell down at Jesus' knees, saying, Depart from me; for I am a sinful man, O Lord." (Luke 5:8) So now he has revelation of who God is and so he goes from saying 'Master' to 'Lord'. He fell down at Jesus' knees; that was an act of worship and reverence, meaning having respect to an authority that is greater than you. Simon Peter reverenced Jesus; this miracle did it; sometimes it takes certain experiences in life for people to see who God really is. Some people have to go through life the hard way before they really see that they need a change in life for the better. Some people have to get hurt in life and get misunderstood and put down by people for them to see that they need God to change them.

Jesus says to Simon, "Fear not; from henceforth thou shalt catch men." In the middle of this miracle Jesus had done for these disciples, he was calling their name for ministry. They went from catching fish to catching men and women and causing them to give their lives to Jesus Christ. What you must realize and understand is that God is calling your name; he wants you right now. If you want to take a break from reading this book and give your life to Christ, go right ahead. Call up a person you know that is strong in the Lord and have them lead you to Jesus; or take a Bible and open it up to Romans 10:9 and repent of your sins, meaning ask God to forgive you of your sins and ask him to come into your heart. It is so easy and simple. Make Jesus your Lord and Savior today because God is calling your name. What Jesus was telling him was that he would preach the Gospel and instead of catching fish they would now catch people and catch their souls and win people to Christ through the Gospel of Jesus Christ, which is the Good News. Whatever state you are in, God is calling your name and God is calling you out of your life of sin. You know you want to be free, but you just don't know how to go about being free; so why not try Jesus? You have tried everything else and nothing you tried work, so I dare you to try Jesus today. I dare you right now where you are to just start calling on the name of Jesus. Maybe you don't say his name a lot, but today is a new start for you and a new chapter in your life, so start calling on his name right now until something happens for you.

CHAPTER ELEVEN

A RENEWED MIND

– Romans 12:1-2 –

The only thing that can renew your mind is the Word of God. The Bible says in 2Timothy 2:15, "Study to show thyself approved unto God, a workman that needeth not to be ashamed, rightly dividing the word of truth." The word of truth is the Word of God. You must understand that you don't have to be a preacher to study God's holy Word. The only way you can defeat the enemy is with the Word of God. You cannot defeat the enemy walking in the flesh. You can only defeat the enemy living a life that is pleasing to God. You cannot rightly divide the word of God if you don't study the Word of truth, which is the Word of God. There are so many Christians that are still prisoners in their own minds. A lot of them only hear and get in the Word of God on Sundays and only when it is convenient for them. In Romans 12:1, Apostle Paul offers a solution; he says, "I beseech you therefore, brethren, by the mercies of God, that ye present your bodies a living sacrifice, holy, acceptable unto God, which is your reasonable service." The key phrase here is the mercies of God. What Paul is saying is that you have to offer your body as a living sacrifice daily, not only when it is convenient for you. You have to be pleasing to God, not just on Sundays or when something bad happens, but you have to be pleasing to God at all times.

Paul goes on to say, "And be not conformed to this world: but be ye transformed by the renewing of your mind, that ye may prove what is that good, and acceptable, and perfect, will of God." (Romans 12:2) Once your mind has been renewed, you then begin to know Christ Jesus. I have discovered that it is hard to walk in the newness of God if you are harboring unforgiveness in your heart, hating people who have wronged you, or you are jealous of other people's successes. If you possess those types of attributes, then it is impossible for your mind to be renewed. You must realize that people who are not walking in forgiveness to other people are the kind of people who really don't know God. If you want to know God then you must develop a prayer life and get in God's Word. You may say you don't understand the Word of God, but there are so many different kinds of Bibles now that break down what the Word is saying, so that you are without excuse. To know God is to know forgiveness; forgiveness is God. In order to have a renewed mind, you must walk in forgiveness. There will be waves and storms in life, but forgiveness can calm the storm. It is the Holy Spirit that can cause you to forgive. I truly challenge anyone who is walking in unforgiveness or who has an issue with someone in your life; if you truly want to inherit eternal life and go to heaven, then you must release it and give it to God. The voice of God in his Word will always lead you to righteousness. It is only the Word of God that can transform and change your mind. I encourage you to get into God's Word daily and spend time with God and commune and converse with God. You make time for your job; you make time for your family; whatever it is that is important to you make time for it. Why don't you make time for God? He deserves your love as well. He died on an old rugged cross for you.

What you have to realize is that where you are now is a result of what you have done in the past. If you want to change the way your life is now, then you must change your sowing. "Whatsoever a man soweth, that shall he also reap. For he that soweth to his flesh shall of the flesh reap corruption; but he that soweth to the Spirit shall of the Spirit reap life everlasting." (Galatians 6:7-8) It is a natural law to reap what you sow. For example, if you gossip about your friends, you will lose their friendship eventually. If you continue to drink excessive wine and alcohol, you will become addicted to alcohol. If you have sexual intercourse outside of marriage, you will become sexually immoral. These are the things that make you unclean in God's sight. If you start gambling with your money, then you will eventually become a gambler and get addicted to it. These are the things that make you unclean in God's sight.

You have the ability to be successful, and you will be successful, if you keep God first. You can make it. You can accomplish anything you want to accomplish if you get in God's divine will and renew your mind. There is nothing on this earth that you cannot accomplish. God has designed this earth so you can do anything you want to do. If you want your own business, then you can do it. Whatever you want to achieve, you can achieve it. I encourage you in the Lord to just reach up and grab what God has for you. You can make it. I believe in you, but you must believe in yourself as well. Go ahead; go for it. You can do it I know you can. Just renew your mind with the Word of God. I know you can change, but you have to believe and know that you can change. God wants to release you into your destiny and into your future, but your mind has to be renewed. Once God releases your blessings to you, then you must be able to maintain your blessings. The reason why so many people are not in their destiny and future is because their minds have not been renewed and God is waiting for them to renew their minds with the Word of God. Once your mind is renewed, then God begins to release into your life what he has ordained for your life. Say yourself, "God Release it! God do it!" God wants to do the supernatural in your life. The only way the supernatural can be done in your life is that you have to stand still and let God be God in your life. God wants to call you to do something supernaturally that you cannot do just in your flesh. God calls ordinary people to do extraordinary things.

Each person that is reading this book is ordained and being set up for greatness. Yes, little old you has been destined for greatness. I believe in you and I know you will make it because of what God says about you, but you must believe in yourself. Someone can tell you all day that you can make it, but until you believe it for yourself and act on it in faith, it will not manifest or happen for you. No one reading this book is a failure; I don't care what your momma or your daddy told you when you were little, I don't care if you were molested, abused, mistreated, talked about, persecuted, or where you were raised, you are not a failure. Even if your marriage is terrible, you are not a failure. Even if you are not financially stable, you are still not a failure. God did not create you to fail; God created you to succeed on this earth. You can and will make it because of our Lord and Savior Jesus Christ. God is a God of the supernatural and God has an infinite mindset, meaning that there is no limit to how he thinks or what he can do. Even today, God still can work miracles and he is doing it for his people.

The reason why the disciples could not walk into their full potential when they were with Jesus was because of their mindset and because their minds had not yet been renewed. After they received the Holy Spirit, their lives were never the same. Once your mind has been renewed by the Word of God, then you can go to the next dimension or level in God. Jesus Christ is calling you to come out of your comfort zone. In order to come out of your comfort zone it takes a sacrifice; that is what God wants you to do for him is to make sacrifices for him. "The harvest truly is plenteous, but the laborers are few." (Matthew 9:37) God is calling for you to labor for the kingdom; God is calling you off of the pew and calling you to do a work; to work in the Ministry, to work in the body of Christ. There is a call on your life. Now when I say there is a call on your life, I am not saying that you are called to preach. There is a call to ministry in what God has given you and placed into your spirit, but you must be prepared and trained before you can walk into it. With God, there has to be preparation before presentation. Once there has been preparation, then there is presentation. What I have noticed is that people don't want to be trained or prepared. What happens is they go out into the field of ministry unprepared and then they make a mess. There has to be preparation and there must be a process and a development into ministry.

The disciples had to be developed; they walked with and trained with Jesus three and half years before they went forth. Because they went through the process, they later became Apostles and great preachers of the Gospel. They didn't rush the process. Some people think they can go on out there because they are of an old age, but just because you are of an old age, still doesn't make you ready for ministry. Our timing isn't God's timing and an old age doesn't make you spiritually mature. "And be renewed in the spirit of your mind." (Ephesians 4:23) In other words, you are no longer where you used to be; you are no longer in sin. You have been bought with a price; you have been redeemed by the blood of Jesus Christ. You have been dipped in the blood; you have been smothered with his blood and you have been dipped in his resurrection. Your mind is being washed by the blood of Jesus. Nail that unforgiveness to the cross. Nail that jealousy and envy to the cross because it will only keep your mind in bondage. You can never see who God really is in your life until you renew your mind.

CHAPTER TWELVE

STOP CRITICIZING

– Luke 6:37-42 –

Jesus teaches about criticizing others. The word 'criticize' means to find fault or to stress the faults. We are living in a world where people criticize each other so much. God showed me that if you are critical rather than compassionate, you in turn also will receive criticism. I must be honest and say that there is so much criticism in the church. When one person falls into sin, then people want to be critical and judgmental. "If a man be overtaken in a fault, ye which are spiritual, restore such a one in the spirit of meekness; considering thyself, lest thou also be tempted." (Galatians 6:1) Some Christians who God has delivered and set free have forgotten where God brought them from and they get so judgmental to everyone else. A forgiving spirit demonstrates that a person has received the Lord's forgiveness. A person that doesn't forgive only shows that they truly don't know God. An individual who knows God will forgive and release out of their heart and spirit the hurt that another individual has caused them. I believe that a person that is always judging others about their sins only shows that they have baggage in their lives.

For an example, the Pharisees were always judging Jesus and people in general. Jesus exposed them; he knew they had a lot of unconfessed sin in their lives. The Bible says in 1John that perfect love casts out fear. If someone is not perfected in love to God's people, then it only signifies that there may be unresolved issues in their lives that they have not dealt with and have hid. I am not trying to hurt anyone's feelings, but I don't want people to be so judgmental until they miss out on what God has for them. No one is perfect; not even the preacher and leaders. We all have issues and individual struggles. Jesus says, "Judge not, and ye shall not be judged." (Luke 6:37) When Jesus speaks, he speaks for a particular reason and for a particular purpose. When you judge, there will always be somebody there to judge you as well. God is calling his people to be tenderhearted towards each other and to operate in the spirit of compassion. God deals with each person differently. Some people get delivered instantly; for others it is a process, so we have no right to judge them. The very person that you are looking down on and judging, God could raise up right in your face and call them to be a powerful and anointed preacher. I say that because I am one who God has raised up. I was judged; I was hurt; I was talked about; I was put down by so-called friends; family members talked about me and told all of my business; people persecuted me; people turned their backs on me and said I would never amount to anything; but look at what God has done. God reached down and grabbed a little young man like me who had dreams of playing basketball; he delivered me, set me free, filled me with the Holy Ghost and called me to preach, to be an Evangelist, and to Pastor God's people. That is why I don't judge anyone and I have compassion on God's people who are struggling. I know I used to be there to as well.

I love God's people with all of my heart. I want to tell everyone out there that is reading this book that God loves you and no matter how deep in sin you are, you can come out and still be used by God. You can still be saved by the powerful hand of God. God can take a prostitute and turn her into a world renowned evangelist. God can take a crack head and turn him into a Pastor. God can take someone that has lost their mind and call them to preach the Gospel; that was me. Look at what God has done. I want to take the time and tell the readers that I love you so much. I really do; I love you. I don't care what kind of sin you are in; I don't like the sin because I have to hate what God hates and God does hate sin, but I love God's people. I love you so much. If your dad doesn't tell you he loves you, I love you and God loves you. I believe in you. I really do love you with the love of Jesus Christ. I believe in you. I don't care what your addiction is, I love you anyway and I pray that God will bring you out of it. Only Jesus Christ has the ability to judge.

There are a lot of people who say they have the gift of discernment, but if you are around them for a while, you will see them acting in the flesh. What I have realized about discernment is that you can only have the God-given discernment if you walk in love. There is no way you can have Godly discernment if you are holding on to unforgiveness; it is impossible. If you don't walk in love towards everyone, then you don't have true discernment. The Pharisees thought they had discernment, but they were evil religious leaders. Jesus had the discernment to see them for who they really were because he walked in pure love. You cannot have the gift of discernment if you don't walk in love to all of God's people. The enemy will let you deceive yourself and make you think you have the gift of discernment, but if you don't walk in love or are holding on to unforgiveness, then you really don't have discernment. Discernment doesn't just see all the bad in people. You have to walk in love like Jesus did. God showed me that you cannot walk in discernment when you are jealous and prideful because true discernment comes from God. God won't give a gift to someone who is jealous and prideful.

What I want you to understand is that you have to have the love of God towards your fellow brothers and sisters in Christ, towards the world and towards those who have wronged you in the past. God wants to win the lost souls through the believers. He wants to win your enemies through you as well. You are to possess the fruit of the Holy Spirit and that is what God wants to see in your life. The Bible says in Galatians 5:22, "The fruit of the Spirit is love, joy, peace, longsuffering, gentleness, goodness, faith, meekness, temperance." A believer who possesses all of those attributes can definitely have discernment. Discernment is based on love. It is not to just see negative things on people and to look down on them and to make you look superior. There are people that have just gotten saved and they need to be discipled and not talked about or put down; deliverance at times can be a process for some people. Once you get in the Word of God and you become conscious of what is right and wrong, then God will began to hold you accountable because you are no longer on milk but you are eating steaks and meats. You must know that if you are critical towards others then you yourself will also be criticized. The Lord is calling you to be compassionate towards the world and towards your enemies. I challenge you if you are holding on to unforgiveness to release it and let it go; it will keep you out of the kingdom of heaven. God is not calling you to settle for less. God doesn't want you be complacent with where you are now; he has a bigger and better plan for your life. If you treat others generously, graciously and compassionately, then these qualities will be done unto you as well. You are to love others and not judge them.

There are liars who judge people who smoke. There are gossipers who judge people who have sex out of marriage. In God's eyes, it is all sin. There are people who judge people who are not married but living together; yes that is sin, but sin is sin. God is calling us to restore and not judge. I want to see all of God's people receive what God has for them. As a preacher of the Gospel, I will show mercy and love towards God's people and not be so quick to judge them, but restore them. Your past does not dictate where you are headed because your past has become a testimony. I don't care what happened in your past or what the devil has thrown your way, it is time for you to tell the devil that you are more than a conqueror in Christ Jesus. The greater your testimony, the greater your anointing and the greater your ministry. God will take someone with a past that was so messed up and God will choose that person and qualify them for ministry. He will miraculously and supernaturally intervene in their life and raise them up to do awesome things in the kingdom of

God. God takes people that man will give up on. One thing I realize is that man will give up on you, but God will never give up on you. You must understand and know that what you do now will dictate how your future will be. You can set the tone and pace of your future by how you live your life now. The Pharisees and religious leaders were hypocrites. The Pharisee spirit is around today. A hypocrite is a person who puts on religious behavior in order to gain attention, approval, acceptance, or admiration from others. I am not trying to judge nobody, but I will say that if you fall in any one of those attributes of this definition, then that is a dangerous place to be in. That definitely means you are prideful. God is looking for people who are humble, meek in spirit and really love and care about God's people. Instead of walking in deception, seek and strive to walk in love. Don't be so quick to criticize a person that God can take and raise up right in your midst and use that person for the glory of God.

CHAPTER THIRTEEN

NAIL YOURSELF TO THE CROSS

– Matthew 16:21-27 –

As a believer, you should learn to nail yourself to the cross and nail your issues to the cross. Jesus died because we were in danger of eternal punishment. Thank God that by him sending his one and only Son Jesus, we now have a shot at heaven. (John 3:16) You should learn to nail your yokes to the cross, your burdens to the cross, and your trials and tribulations to the cross. That is what Jesus died for; you must know and understand that there is always room at the cross for you. You must understand that the enemy wants you to think that God doesn't want anything to do with you, but that is only a trick of the enemy. God loves you and he wants to give you your real blessings. One thing God showed me was that a camouflage blessing comes from the enemy and it only lasts for a season. A true blessing comes from God and it lasts for eternity. Anything that satan gives you does not last, but what God gives you does last. The only thing that will last forever that satan can give you is being in hell, where he and his demons are going. When you go to hell, then it will last forever. You will be in torment and pain forever and ever and it will never stop.

In this passage of scripture, Jesus is prophesying about his death and he was talking to his disciples about how he must go to Jerusalem and suffer. Peter pulls him to the side and rebukes Jesus. Jesus, full of the Holy Ghost, rebukes Peter in love. There comes a time that you need to be rebuked, but the way to rebuke is in love. When Peter rebuked Jesus, it was only because Peter had no revelation of what Jesus Christ had to go through for this whole entire world. As a believer and even as a nonbeliever, you never know when a difficult time in your life will come. That is why it is important that you have a relationship with Jesus and be under the blood of Jesus Christ. You will need a Savior to carry you through whatever it is that you will go through in this life. That is also why you have to nail yourself to the cross; so you can be ready for anything that may come your way in this life. One of the many ways you can nail yourself to the cross is through getting saved and giving your life to Jesus Christ. If you will give up your life for Jesus Christ or give up your sinful lifestyle for Jesus Christ, then you will inherit eternal life through Jesus Christ. What God is calling you to do is to give your issues, burdens and your problems to him. You have been trying to work things out in your life without him, but he has an out-stretched hand waiting for you to give it to him. He is a problem bearer, a burden bearer and a problem solver. If you truly love Jesus Christ and if you are tired of the lifestyle you are in, you will nail yourself to the cross for the better. Does God know your personal e-mail address? Do you talk to him daily? Do you spend time with him or do you just call on him when you want something from him? Does God even know your name? When was the last time you logged on to God's website of prayer? When was the last time you logged in to God's website of the Word?

I am telling you that he is waiting for you to pull up his website and he is calling for you to sign up and register today. It is time for you to bring glory to God by giving him your life. If you have given your life to him, but have fallen away a little, now is your time to come back to him and nail yourself to the cross. If you nail yourself to the cross, then I promise your life will never be the same. You must know and understand that God loves you so much; he loves you so much until he sacrificed his one and only Son Jesus Christ just for you. All Jesus Christ wants from you is that one-on-one relationship with him where you and he will spend time with each other. Jesus says, "If any man will come after me, let him deny himself, and take up his cross, and follow me." (Matthew 16:24) When Jesus used this example of a person taking up their cross, they knew what he meant because crucifixion was a common Roman method of execution. You must realize and understand that Jesus already went through the execution for you; all you have to do is take up your cross and follow Jesus for the rest of your life. You can nail yourself to the cross by asking Jesus Christ to come into your life and repenting from all of your sins. Jesus doesn't care how much you have sinned; he is much more concerned about you changing your life and following after him. You have to be willing to sacrifice your life and body for the sake of Jesus.

When you think about it, people sacrifice everyday for things in this world. People make sacrifices to become millionaires. People make sacrifices for jobs, for money and for people they love. Why not make that commitment and sacrifice for a Savior who died on the cross for your sins? After you receive Jesus Christ into your life, you have total access to the Holy Spirit and everything that Jesus has to offer you. Some of the things that Jesus has to offer you are salvation, the Holy Spirit and heaven. There is something about the Holy Spirit; the Holy Spirit will bring you peace in your life when all things are not so good in your life. When someone does something really bad to hurt you, the Holy Spirit will give you the strength to not seek revenge or to take matters into your own hands. When you find yourself in a bad situation and someone is doing something to hurt you, just ask the Holy Spirit to give you peace and nail it to the cross. When you have access to the Holy Spirit you have authority over the enemy. The Greek word for authority is exousia, which means delegated authority. For example, a cop's badge represents authority because of his position; he has the ability to use his power, which in Greek is dunamis, which is miraculous power. The cop can use his power when he has to. God reveled this to me and showed me that the authority represents the Holy Spirit and the power represents the Word of God. The Holy Spirit has authority that is given by God and the Word of God is powerful.

Jesus says in Matthew 16:24, "If any man will come after me, let him deny himself, and take up his cross, and follow me." I have realized that this is difficult for some people to do. Some people are so stuck on the things of this world and the things of the flesh, rather than the things of the Spirit. God is calling us to be of the things of the Spirit and not things of the flesh. People rather would be a leader than a follower. God is raising up followers in the kingdom to do a work in this last and evil day. Jesus Christ is saying that it is not about you, but it is about him. If you follow him, then you have to die to yourself spiritually and crucify your flesh. Jesus is saying that to follow him is to gain eternal life in heaven.

Jesus states, "For whosoever will save his life will lose it: and whosoever will lose his life for my sake shall find it." (Matthew 16:25) If you are willing to let go of the sin that has you in bondage for the sake of Jesus Christ, then you will inherit eternal life. If you become a disciple of Jesus Christ over the world, then you will reap all of the blessings that Jesus Christ has to offer you. Real discipleship requires real commitment. If you are truly willing to be a true disciple, then it takes letting go of the things of the flesh to be the disciple that God has called you to be. God is calling you to nail every addiction that you have to the cross; every evil work and every work of the flesh, Jesus is calling you to nail it to the cross. Jesus says, "For what is a man profited, if he shall gain the whole world, and lose his own soul?" (Matthew 16:26) That statement is so powerful by itself. So many people die empty. One thing you must realize is that no matter how much money you have or acquire on this earth, once you die you cannot take anything with you.

Jesus says, "Seek ye first the kingdom of God, and his righteousness; and all these things shall be added unto you." (Matthew 6:33) There must be a balance; God must be first in your life because you cannot do anything without Jesus Christ being Lord over your life. I am so glad that I realized at a young age that I can do nothing without Jesus Christ. Jesus is my all and my everything. Apart from him, I am nothing. I need him every minute and every hour. I especially have a heart for the young people because the devil is destroying our young people. I hope and pray that young people will read this book and that they will see that there is an enemy out there that doesn't want them to make it into the kingdom of heaven. Nowadays, it seems more young people are dying than old people. Young people are getting caught up into secular hip hop, secular rap music, gangs, sex out of marriage, drugs and alcohol; it shouldn't be that way. I want to tell the parents that you should be honest with your kids and make it so that they can trust you, confide in you, and talk to you about anything. Young kids are growing up fast today and they are exposed to a lot more things than when we were growing up. As a parent, you must stay close to God for the sake of your children. As of right now, you can choose to nail yourself to the cross. If you start to look at things from an eternal point of view, then it begins to transform your view of life and gives you an eternal mindset. The only way you can have an eternal mindset is by your mind being renewed by the Word of God. The Holy Spirit always wants you to receive revelation of who God is.

Jesus says, "But the Comforter, which is the Holy Ghost, whom the Father will send in my name, he shall teach you all things, and bring all things to your remembrance, whatsoever I have said unto you." (John 14:26) What you must know and understand is that in order for the Word to be brought back to your remembrance, you must take time out and study the Word of God. Jesus just isn't going to show you who he is without you seeking him. You have to show Jesus that you are serious about developing a relationship with him. Some people who want to be preachers or pastors get caught up in just wanting a title, but not wanting the one-on-one relationship with Jesus. In order to have an effective ministry, you must have a relationship with Jesus Christ. When you let go of your sinful lifestyle for Jesus Christ, then you gain a life of Christ and eternal life; that is a great blessing. The Holy Spirit is what makes us nail ourselves to the cross and keeps us on the cross. I want you to realize that no matter how deep you are in sin, you can still nail yourself to the cross today. Jesus is waiting for you and he is ready to wrap his righteous and holy arms around you. Make him yours today by nailing yourself to the cross.

CHAPTER FOURTEEN

IF YOU ONLY KNEW THE GIFT

– John 4:1-26 –

This passage of scripture starts off talking about the Pharisees hearing about the gift, who is Jesus, baptizing and gaining more disciples than John the Baptist. It was not the gift, who is Jesus, who baptized, but it was his disciples who baptized. (John 4:1-2) When Jesus learned of this, he departed and went on to Galilee. Jesus had to go through Samaria and he came to a town in Samaria called Sychar. Jesus was tired, so he sat down by the well. It was about the sixth hour, but Jesus, who is a gift, had a divine appointment with a spiritually lost woman. Jesus Christ is ready to make an appointment with you right now. Perhaps you are like this Samaritan woman and you think that Jesus doesn't want anything to do with you. I must tell you that you are the kind of person that Jesus wants to deal with.

You may be in the pit of sin, but I tell you that Jesus wants to deal with you right where you are. Jesus had to minister to this Samaritan woman, who had no revelation of who Jesus was. All she knew was that Jesus was a Jew and that Jews didn't associate themselves with Samaritans. This Samaritan woman came to draw water, and Jesus says, "Give me to drink." (John 4:7) Jesus is the gift and he is very different and very unique in a special way. The Samaritan woman said to Jesus, "How is it that thou, being a Jew, askest drink of me, which am a woman of Samaria? For the Jews have no dealings with the Samaritans." (John 4:9) What she didn't realize was that she was talking to the gift of life, the gift of healing, the gift of destiny, and the gift of promise. Jesus says, "If thou knewest the gift of God, and who it is that saith to thee, Give me to drink; thou wouldest have asked of him, and he would have given thee living water." (John 4:10) He is basically offering this woman salvation and spiritual life. This woman is spiritually dead and Jesus is trying to show this woman that Jews may not like the Samaritans, but even though he is a Jew, he is called to save everyone and he is on a divine assignment. This Samaritan woman thinks Jesus is talking from a fleshly perspective, but Jesus is talking from a spiritual perspective. He is seeking to give this woman eternal life and salvation through himself. He was offering her the living water that would cause her to never spiritually thirst again. He was giving her the true and living water that could quench her thirst spiritually.

Too many times, people are drinking the wrong kind of water spiritually. They are drinking the water of depression, the water of doubt, the water of fear, the water of hate, the water of jealousy and envy, the water of gambling, or the water of lying; those are all waters of the flesh. God is seeking and trying to bring people out of all that bondage. People go to church Sunday after Sunday and they are still thirsty. So many people are looking for things to quench their thirst, but only God can quench your thirst spiritually. You can try everything else that you think that can satisfy you, but you will come to the conclusion that only Jesus Christ can satisfy you spiritually. Some women look for men to quench their thirst, but then they get hurt and wonder why they got hurt. The reason is because they were drinking the wrong kind of water. Ask yourself this question: what kind of water are you drinking that is spiritually keeping you away from God? Jesus was offering the Samaritan woman living water; the water that would deliver her; the water that would set her free; the kind of water that would make her whole. Church alone cannot quench your thirst spiritually. You have to do more than just show up at service for your spirit to be right. You have to develop a relationship with Jesus Christ and then that will quench your thirst spiritually. You have to spend time with God like you spent time when people when you were in sin. When you are in sin, you devote a lot of time to it. So once you give your life to Jesus, you then have to devote time with him as well. When you come to church, you should come to church not just because it is the right thing to do. Seeing the church only as an event keeps God from revealing himself to you and it keeps you in bondage. Coming to church and experiencing the power of the Holy Spirit destroys the yokes and sets you free from the powers of satan. You must know that you cannot recognize Jesus by cognitive understanding, but Jesus can only be revealed through and by the manifestation of the Holy Ghost. In Matthew 16:13-20, it was revealed to Peter by the Holy Spirit that Jesus Christ was the Messiah which means, the Anointed One.

In this dialogue between the Samaritan woman and Jesus, the Samaritan woman asked where she could get this drink from. I believe that one of the reasons why Jesus talked to her was because he wanted to offer her salvation and break this racism between the Samaritan and Jews. God is calling for you to be a witness for Jesus. It is easy to go to church and witness to believers, but God wants the drug dealer saved. God wants to the prostitute saved. God wants the drug user and crack head saved, delivered and set free. This Samaritan woman asked, "Are thou greater than our father Jacob?"

(John 4:12) The Samaritan woman was in error in calling Jacob her father; she really didn't possess the authority to regard herself or even the Samaritans as descendants of Jacob. Jesus boldly says, "Whosoever drinketh of this water shall thirst again: But whosoever drinketh of the water that I shall give him shall never thirst." (John 4:13-14) In other words, Jesus was talking about himself and giving people the gift of salvation and a chance for eternal life in him.

God wants you to have the drink of righteousness, joy, peace, happiness, love, gentleness, and patience; these are some of the many things that God wants you to have. The only way you can have these things is to give your life to him. What kind of drink are you willing to give Jesus? Jesus gave this Samaritan woman the kind of drink that she would never spiritually thirst again. Are you willing to give Jesus the drink of honesty, the drink of faithfulness, and the drink of love towards God and other people? In this passage of scripture, God showed me that as believers, you cannot just drink from just any source; the drink must be a sound doctrine, which is the doctrine of Christ. You must take the drink that Jesus has to offer you. If you spiritually drink from Jesus, then you will never thirst again. If you be like the Samaritans and drink from the well, then you will always keep having to go back to the well and will always get thirsty again.

If you spiritually drink from the well of this world, looking for the things of this world to satisfy you, then you will never be satisfied. When you eat, the food you eat cannot carry you for a long time, but you have to eat every day. If you drink today, it is not enough to carry you to another day; you have to drink every day. That is how it is in the Spirit; you have to read God's Word every day and you have to pray every day. That is what this story is about; receiving what Jesus Christ has to offer you so that you will never spiritually thirst again and that you will receive the gift of life. All Jesus wants you to do is give your life to him and surrender. If you give your life to him, then you will be protected and that qualifies you for salvation. All he wants to do is pour out the fountain of love in your life so your life will be transformed. Just allow him to love you, allow him to deliver you, allow him to change your life forever. When Jesus said that salvation is from the Jews, he meant that only through the Jewish Messiah would the whole world find salvation. God had promised that through the Jewish race, the whole earth would be blessed. (Genesis 12:3) The Old Testament prophets had called the Jews to be the light to the other nations. They had predicted the Messiah's coming. The Samaritan woman may have known these passages and was expecting the Messiah, but she didn't realize she was already talking to the Messiah. As for you, Jesus is waiting for you. He is waiting for you to surrender to him. He is waiting for you to draw closer to him. He is waiting for you to get saved. If you are saved, he is waiting for you to get to work in ministry. You may be going through, but you have power in the spirit. You may have gotten a divorce or may be separated, but Jesus is still with you. You may have issues, but Jesus is still with you and waiting for you to call upon his name and make that change and to renew your mind with the Word of God. You must know and understand that as long as you are a believer, you have power in the Spirit to overcome any obstacle in life. If you only knew the gift, who is Jesus Christ our Lord and Savior. It doesn't matter what your past is or even what you are still in, Jesus is waiting to be your gift today.

CHAPTER FIFTEEN

I HAVE TO GET TO MY DESTINY

– Mark 14:32-42 –

Jesus is driven to the garden of Gethsemane, a place where he faced who he really is. He was getting ready to take upon the sins of the world. He was driven to deal with who he really is, and that is the Christ. At this place called Gethsemane, he begins to deal with the ultimate task that was ahead of him. In this place, he has opposition with the issue of him going through this horrendous process to save and redeem humanity. This is a place that the Messiah, or the Christ, knew he would end up, but when he's faced with this opposition, he gets what you would call distressed. In the midst of this opposition, he finds strength and confidence in the horrific journey he was about to face. What God is calling us to do is to deal with and face opposition. As long as you live on the face of this earth, you will have opposition at some point and time in your life. That is something that you cannot stop or hinder in your life; it is coming and will happen no matter what. The word opposition means to strive against or to place against something. The whole time Christ was on this earth, he was being faced with opposition. It is opposition that caused him to persevere through it all. Going through opposition can and will strengthen you and prepare you for your destiny. When Joseph was thrown into the pit and his brothers plotted against him, it only prepared him for his destiny.

When Jesus was being tempted while he was fasting for forty days and forty nights, being in the wilderness, and satan was bringing so much opposition his way, he persevered. He said that man shall not live by bread alone, but by every word that proceeds out of the mouth of God. (Matthew 4:1-4) If you stand on the Word of God and have faith in the Word of God, then it will definitely get you to your destiny. Jesus said to his disciples, "Sit ye here, while I shall pray." (Mark 14:32) That implies something; they were told to sit while he went and prayed. How many times has God instructed you to do something and you didn't take heed to what God had said? Many times, God will test you in the small things to see if you will be faithful in the little things. When you become faithful in the small things, he will trust you with greater things and greater tasks.

For example, God can't trust you with a million dollars if you are not a faithful tither. God is seeking to drive you into purpose. In him driving you into your purpose, it causes you to mature in the knowledge of Jesus Christ our Lord. One of the best ways for you to grow in the knowledge of the Lord is through prayer. Prayer is a powerful weapon. As a believer, you should always have an attitude of prayer. It is in prayer that you get to see who God really is to you. Prayer will strengthen you to deal with life's obstacles. Prayer may not always change the situations all the time and it may not always release the opposition in your life, but one thing I do know is that prayer can change you. Prayer can change you and there are also lots of times that prayer can change the situations as well.

CHAPTER SIXTEEN

DON'T MAKE THE KINGDOM OF GOD A SECRET

– Mark 4:1-25 –

In the book of Mark, he gets right into who Jesus Christ is. He deals with Christology, which is the study of Christ. Mark deals with the life of Christ and he digs right into the deepness of who Christ is. When you deal with Christology, you will find out how Christ operated and carried himself in several situations. In this parable, you will find that Jesus is at the beginning of his earthly ministry and he is working miracles and wonders. Jesus was teaching in the synagogues healing lepers and casting out devils. Now, Jesus is at the sea side teaching in parables. The Greek word for parable means a proverb, figure, or fictitious narrative. If it is a fictitious narrative, then it implies that Jesus was using seemingly real-life stories to convey a spiritual truth to his hearers. Jesus began to teach or instruct by the sea side and there gathered to him a great multitude, meaning a lot of people gathered. Jesus says, "There went out a sower to sow." (Mark 4:3) The question is, who is the sower and what does the sower sow? When Jesus taught in parables, his parables had one main point. When teaching or preaching on Jesus' parables, you must be careful not to add to them and only teach what Jesus was intending to impart into his hearers. Even while Jesus is teaching this parable, he is sowing the word. This is his doctrine, meaning his instruction, and he's sowing the word. John 1:1 says, "In the beginning was the Word, and the Word was with God, and the Word was God." If Jesus is the Word, since he was in the beginning, then that means that while Jesus was sowing the Word concerning this parable of the sower, then that means Jesus was speaking of himself. The seed was the Word of God. Jesus is the Word. This parable is talking about a sower sowing the Word and Jesus is sowing this parable to his disciples and the many people that are listening. By him teaching in parables, it somewhat concealed the spiritual truth from the ones who didn't want to receive Jesus, such as the Pharisees and the religious leaders. Since this parable is referring to the Word, then that means Jesus is referring to himself and is sowing of himself. Why? Because he is the Living Word. Jesus is teaching this parable to minister to his audience that they would have received what he had to say. However, many people did not understand what he was teaching. Jesus says, "As he sowed, some fell by the way side, and the fowls of the air came and devoured it up." (Mark 4:4)

The Greek word for fowl means a flying animal. From a spiritual perspective, are you going to let the fowls of this world keep you out of the house of God? Are you going to let the fowls of this corrupt world keep you from serving God with a whole heart? Are you going to let the fowls of the earth keep you out of heaven? Are the things of this world worth you missing out on what God has for you spiritually, financially, emotionally, and health wise? The sower sowed and some fell by the way side. To me a way sider is someone who has no root in God. Just as soon as something bad happens, they turn their back on God and want to blame God for the negative cares of this life. I encourage you to never fall into that category. If you do, then God still loves you. There are so many people that don't even believe in God who are atheists, but God still loves the atheist. God does not approve of a person not believing in him, but he is always there to reveal himself to you. Even if you are a way sider reading this book, then you still have hope. God has led you to read this book for a reason. I want you to know that I love you so much;

I love you with the love of God and I believe in you. I want you to know that you can make it and you are destined for greatness. Never try and be great and successful without Jesus Christ. True success begins with you establishing a relationship with Jesus Christ.

There were so many people that hurt me and turned their back on me and said I would never make it. People talked about me and church people even hurt me, but I never gave up on God. Now I am preaching all over, writing one of the many books that I will write and pastoring; all because of the grace of God that was distributed from God. I want to let you know that no matter how deep in sin you are, God can bring you out. God can change anyone that wants to be changed. I want you to know that I believe in you. I know you will make it. I have confidence in you, but you must believe and have confidence in yourself. I am not here to criticize any one. I am just exposing the truth. What I have realized is that this world operates on deception. Some people don't want the truth. Sometimes the truth hurts, but the truth is designed for you to face reality. Facing reality is a great thing. When you face your realities, it gives you hope. Face reality today and learn to face the truth and deal with who you really are so God can change your life forever. The way siders, once they are attacked by the fowls of the air, fold up and give up. In other words, when the way siders are attacked by the devil, they give up on God based on what they are going through. Tell yourself to not be a way sider. If you are a way sider, then after reading this chapter, I hope you will seek after the truth, which is the Word of God.

Jesus says, "Some fell on stony ground, where it had not much earth; and immediately it sprang up, because it had no depth of earth." (Mark 4:5) In the Greek, stony is rock like. If it is rock like, then that means it is impossible for a seed to harvest. When a person has a stony, rock like mentality, it is very difficult for the Word of God to penetrate their heart. In order for the sower to receive a harvest from the seeds he has sown, it has to get into some soil. If the seed doesn't get into some soil, then there can be no harvest. God is calling his people to have is a soil like mentality. There are so many people that come to church, but they still possess a stony and rocky like mentality and then there is no change in their lives. Stony and rock-like people have no true relationship with God. They are the kind of people who last but only for a moment and they have no depth in their relationship with God. When you have depth in your relationship with God, it doesn't matter if you are sick in your body, it doesn't matter if you are financially unstable and it doesn't matter what the enemy throws your way. Because you have depth in your relationship with God, you still won't give up on God. When you have that depth in your life with God, there is nothing the devil can throw your way that will cause you to give up on God.

The Bible says, "But when the sun was up, it was scorched; and because it had no root, it withered away." (Mark 4:6) When seeds are sown in a foreign area of the ground and the sun hits them, it scorches them. In the Greek, scorch means burn. That is why people give up on God and leave the church; they have no depth and have no root in God. When people get hurt in the church by the pastor or members of the church and they leave due to that, then it only shows they are not rooted and grounded in the Word of God or their relationship with God. When you are dedicated to God, no matter what anyone does to you in the church, you won't leave the church nor will you give up on God. I have been hurt by many people in the church and I stayed in church and didn't let what people in the church had done to me cause me to walk out on God. Anytime you want to blame God or people for what they have done and what you are going through, then that keeps you from knowing who God really is. People who allow the devil to scorch them or burn them up have no root in Christ Jesus. This sower sowed parts of this seed in unstable places. You must be careful where you sow the Word of God as your seed; everyone will not receive it.

As Jesus went around teaching his doctrine, he was sowing his seed, which is the Word of God. He was sowing of himself because he is the Word. A lot of times he was sowing himself to people who were not rooted in him and who were unstable, but he didn't let that stop him from sowing his seed. In today's world, the Word is being sowed to unstable people who have no root and who are not stable in their walk with God. People who church hop say, "I want to go to a church that is big with a lot of members or that has a lot of things to do there or because that's where everyone else goes." They have no set place where they are active in ministry and they are the ones who have no root in God and they are considered as unstable. I would encourage you to never take advice from a church hopper and don't take advice from a person who is showing no Godly fruit in their lives, even if they proclaim Christianity or proclaim a title. People who are not active in ministry, church hop, or never get stable in ministry don't know their purpose and have no root. They are the ones who are double minded. The Bible says, "A double minded man is unstable in all his ways." (James 1:8) That is why you should pray before making critical decisions. When you pray before doing certain things, it causes you to be patient. Patience is one of the fruits of the Holy Spirit. (Galatians 5:22) It's best to not receive from people who are double minded because Godly wisdom is unusual to a double minded person. A double minded person can never realize who God is unless there is a change by the hand of God. That is why it is important for you to walk with a man or woman of God who is walking in fear of the Lord. A double minded person can't tell you too much at all.

The Bible says, "Some fell among thorns, and the thorns grew up, and choked it, and it yielded no fruit." (Mark 4:7) A thorn is something that causes distress. When the word of God is sown in someone that causes distress, you can look for the Word of God to be choked out of them and they will not possess any type of positive fruit. When a person is distressful, they don't have peace within themselves and they are pessimistic, meaning they are negative and they are not happy. Have you ever been around people who are just so negative that everything that comes out of their mouths is negative? Negative people will really discourage you. You must surround yourself with Christian believers who won't look at the way things look in your life, but will encourage you, speak life to you and let you know that it doesn't matter what it looks like because you are still going to make it and you still have hope.

When the sower is sowing among thorns, you can definitely look for the seeds to not yield a harvest. When a preacher is sowing the Word of God or preaching the Word of God, it won't always fall on good ground. A lot of times it will fall on thorny people or people who are distressful. As a preacher, you still must not lose hope because there are always some people out there who will produce a harvest from the Word of God that preachers are sowing into the lives of God's people. No matter what it looks like or how bad things may get, God is still in control and there is always hope. It may seem like God is not in control based on what people may see in this world, but God is still a winner and in the end, the devil will be defeated. A person that is thorny or distressful will leave the church the same way they came in. In other words, a distressful person will come into the church bound and will leave bound. The church people who are distressful or thorny will cause the world to choke the Word of God from them that they receive from the preacher. Once you hear the Word of God, he expects you to apply it to your life. It is very important that you stay in the church or get in the church when the devil is really coming against you. Some people walk away from God and the church when the devil attacks them, but that only shows that they have no root in God at all. When you have root in God, then no devil or no demon can keep you from serving God and being in the house of God. When you allow the things of the world to keep you out of the house of God, it only exposes you for who you are at that moment and shows that you are producing no positive fruit in God.

The Bible says, "And other fell on good ground, and did yield fruit that sprang up and increased; and brought forth, some thirty, and some sixty, and some a hundred." (Mark 4:8) There are actually people that will receive the Word from the sower. When Jesus was sowing the Word, there were always people that received it and applied it. Anytime the Word of God is sown, there will always be good ground that it will fall on. It will yield fruit in a person; it will spring up in a person and bring increase to that individual that receives it. I want you to be that person that will hear the Word, receive the Word and apply the Word of God. Please don't make the kingdom of God a secret. Make sure you go and share Jesus with someone; perhaps it is with an unsaved family member that you have been working on for years. It may be a coworker you have been praying for, or your loved ones; don't make Jesus a secret and don't be ashamed that you are a Christian. If you are reading this book and you are not a Christian then now is your chance to become a Christian and not make the kingdom of God a secret. Perhaps you may not have gotten saved or gave your life to Christ, but you are at the point where you want to give your life to God, but that sinful addiction is keeping you from giving your life to Christ and you just can't let it go because you like it or it feels good to your flesh. It isn't worth it; you will have to die one day and tomorrow is definitely not promised. Please don't let your addictions cause you to miss out on heaven.

Jesus paints a picture in this parable that entails when the seed, which is the Word of God, is sown, it will fall on different kinds of people; it will hit the way siders, the stony people, the thorny people and also the good grounders. Jesus says to them, "Know ye not this parable? and how then will ye know all parables?" (Mark 4:13) The revelation to why Jesus was asking these questions was because Jesus was teaching them this parable about the Word of God and he knew that if they didn't get this parable about the Word of God, then it would be impossible for them to comprehend or understand the rest of his parables he would give in his teachings.

If you don't understand the Word of God, it will be difficult for you to live by it. People flock to what is familiar to them. People flock to what they understand and what makes them feel good, which isn't always a good thing. The devil will use that against them. Everything that is familiar to you isn't always what you need. The devil can dress up and make something seem like it is a blessing when in fact, it is a curse. Jesus says, "The sower soweth the word. And these are they by the way side, where the word is sown; but when they have heard, satan cometh immediately, and taketh away the word that was sown in their hearts." (Mark 4:14-15) In other words, when you come to church and hear a great word from the Lord, the devil will then come to attack you and to take the word of God that you received from the preacher out of your heart; then you would have forgotten about the word you have received. The devil will try to bring up your past to keep you from serving God, but your past is your past and God doesn't care about your past, so neither should you. The devil is stealing the Word of God from people every day; please don't let him steal the Word of God from you. Pick up your sword and fight; fight with prayer, fight with faith in God believing that God can bring you through any fight and through any test or temptation you will ever face in this life. The devil knows that if he can continue to keep Jesus out of a person's life, they will remain spiritually dead and remain defeated.

Jesus says, "And these are they likewise which are sown on stony ground; who, when they have heard the word, immediately receive it with gladness; And have no root in themselves, and so endure but for a time: afterward, when affliction or persecution ariseth for the word's sake, immediately they are offended." (Mark 4:16-17) In other words, a person can receive the word of God, hear it, enjoy it and say the message was awesome, but when they start being attacked from the devil, the situations of life start to weigh on them and they start going through because of the good word they are getting, they immediately choke up. The revelation to this parable is that it is not just talking about different kinds of people and how they receive the Word of God, but it can be the same person and them being in different stages in their Christian walk. For example, you can believe God for your healing and want God to bless you, but not want to be faithful in the church. You can want God to bless you with a job or finances, but not be faithful in tithing or giving in the church. You can want God to bless you and answer your prayers, but not want to come out of the sinful lifestyle you are presently in; it definitely should not be that way at all.

This parable can be seen in so many different ways. Jesus goes on to say, "And these are they which are sown among thorns; such as hear the word, And the cares of this world, and the deceitfulness of riches, and the lusts of other things entering in, choke the word, and it becometh unfruitful." (Mark 4:18-19) In other words, Jesus is saying that the so-called church people and people who hear the word of God have let the world, the riches of this world, the absurd lifestyles and the sins of this world cause them to turn their back on God and not any longer seek to please God. When you seek to let the things of this world please you rather than God, you have turned your back on God. You may not have turned your back on God verbally, but your actions and your lifestyle have proven that your back is turned on God. Even in you doing that, God still loves you. You must know and understand how much God loves you. If you don't get anything else out of this book, just know that God loves you and I love you as well. That is why I am revealing to you the truth; I love you and I believe in you. You may be deep in sin, but I still love you and I still believe in you. You may be a growing Christian; I love you. You may be a nonbeliever; I still love you and so does God. However, in order to make it into heaven, you must give your life to Jesus. You cannot make it without Jesus. If your heart is into making money and living life without God, then the riches of this world is where your heart is. Some of you want God to bless you so much financially. If God was to actually do it, would it take you out of church? Would it take you away from God? For an unbeliever, would it take you even further away from God and increase your sin the more? Think about that for a second. Jesus says, "And these are they which are sown on good ground; such as hear the word, and receive it, and bring forth fruit, some thirtyfold, some sixty, and some a hundred." (Mark 4:20) The ones in that parable are the ones that not only hear the Word of God, but they apply it to their lives and they bring forth fruit based on them applying the Word of God to their lives. Whatever you do, please make sure you don't make the kingdom of God a secret. Make sure you tell someone about the goodness of Jesus. You just might be saving their life from the Lake of Fire.

CHAPTER SEVENTEEN

IT'S TIME TO COME OUT OF THE TOMB

– Matthew 28:1-7 –

This was a very difficult moment for Jesus' disciples, but what seemingly looked like a defeat was a triumphant moment for every believer who believed in Jesus Christ at that time. Out of all the miracles, healings, and divine acts that Jesus Christ had done, it seemed like it was in vain. Notice I said 'it seemed'. Jesus Christ displayed the agape love (which is Godly love) and also displayed all of his divine attributes and still ended up in a tomb. As I studied the word tomb, I realized that ending up in a tomb isn't always a bad thing. The word tomb in the Greek is mnemeion, which means cenotaph, which means a monument erected in honor of a person. Jesus went in the tomb knowing that he was going to rise and come up out of the tomb. Just because you are having a tomb experience, you have to have the faith in God to know that God is going to bring you out of the tomb alive, just like he did his Son Jesus, who is now Lord and Savior of this world. This is where Joseph, the rich man, chose to bury Jesus because Joseph understood Jesus' worth and who he is. Earlier, in Matthew 27, it talks about how Jesus was mocked by the Roman soldiers; they stripped him and put a scarlet robe on him and it was an old red cloak, such as the Roman soldiers wore. It was an imitation of the scarlet robes which kings and emperors wore. They were basically mocking him because they knew he called himself the Messiah or Son of the Living God. They also put together a crown of thorns and set it on his head; that was a symbolism of the fact that they knew he addressed himself as a king, which he is. Then they put a staff in his right hand and knelt in front of him and mocked him. A staff is a pole, stick or rod. They began to say, "Hail, king of the Jews." They began to spit in his face and took the staff and began to beat him with it multiple times. They beat him on his head again and again and again. This is something that Jesus went through. He went through all of this for you and for me. Jesus still went through this knowing today that people would still reject him and still not live a holy and Godly life for him. Yet he still died and he still went in the tomb just for you. They mutilated his flesh and began to beat him so bad that his flesh started falling off of his body. There were about 200 soldiers there mocking him and beating him. After this horrendous beating and traumatizing moment to his flesh, he is then led away to be crucified. He was led to be crucified at a place called Golgotha, which means a place of the skull.

I declare to you that it is alright if you are in the tomb and going through. It is the tomb that prepares you for what God has for you. Jesus Christ knew he was going to the tomb, but he also had an assurance that he was coming up out of the tomb. Jesus was put in a tomb physically dead, but he came up out of the tomb alive, being no longer subject to death. You may be in your tomb now based on your bad situation. You may have been pronounced dead, not physically, but based on your problems. I serve notice on the devil that God is going to bring you out and see you through. You must have faith like Jesus Christ had and say, "I was put in the tomb dead, but no matter what my situation, no matter what I am going through and no matter what problems I have, I am determined in my spirit that I am coming up out of this tomb alive in Christ Jesus." Notice when Jesus was on the cross suffering and being tormented, the angels were not there. God allowed Jesus to go through this horrific death. Jesus says, "Eli, Eli, lama sabachthani?" which means My God, My God why have you forsaken me?" (Matthew 27:46) Even at that time Jesus was separated from God, God never forsook Jesus. He was just allowing his son Jesus to do what he had called him to do. Notice that God shows up at the tomb.

If you are in a crisis situation, then count it all joy. Sometimes God will let situations get so bad before he shows up just to show you and the devil that he is God. If you are in a situation right now and you don't know how you are going to come out, then still count all joy and know that God is going to manifest himself in the situations that you are experiencing. If you are in the tombs of life, then count it all joy. That means you know God and his angels are about to show up and raise you from the dead and depths of your problems, in God's timing and not your timing. God and his angels are about to raise you up out of your problems if you just have faith in him. In Matthew 27:62, there were guards placed at the tomb. The chief priests and the Pharisees remembered that Jesus said he would be raised from the dead, so they had the tomb sealed. Theologically speaking, you cannot keep God incarnate (meaning having a bodily form) bound by earthly specifications. The guards were posted at the tomb; to me, guards represent the enemy and so do the Pharisees and chief priests. God may allow you to be in your tomb of life, seal you in your tomb, and then put your enemies at the post of your tomb so God can get the glory out of your situation. God is going to bring you out of your tomb in the midst of your enemies. God is going to allow all of that so you can draw closer to him and show the devil that he has messed with the wrong individual.

The Bible says, "Weeping may endure for a night, but joy cometh in the morning." (Psalm 30:5) Yes, yes, yes…let your enemies stand at the door post and watch you suffer in your tomb because it is only a matter of time before you are going to bust up out of your tomb with the victory. Hallelujah!!!! Victory is yours; just believe it, receive and claim it!!! It is time for you to come out of your tomb! Let people talk about you, gossip about you, lie on you and as a matter of fact let the enemy bury you alive. In a matter of time, you are going to bust up out of your tomb with much more power in the Holy Ghost than you ever had before. Show the enemy that you may be in the tomb, but while you are in this tomb, your faith is being built up, your love for people is increasing, you are getting in the Word of God more, and you are showing yourself friendly to God's people and to ungodly people as well. Some of you believers know you are called to preach and you have been waiting. I must tell you, keep serving God and remain faithful in a blessed ministry. Before you can be a pastor or a leader, you must know what it is like to be a follower. My Bishop says that when you want to be a pastor, people are going to want to know who you followed, who you trained under, who ordained you and if you were faithful to a ministry. You can't jump from the pew of the church to the pulpit; it is a process. With ministry, you cannot skip the process. I have heard about so many people who pay to be licensed and ordained through websites online; they just go online and pay for license and to be ordained. What those people who are doing that don't realize is that you cannot purchase the anointing. There are other things you can fake, but you can't buy the anointing. Just because your friend or family member is a preacher, doesn't mean you are called to be one. That is something God has to call you to do. If you have to pay to be ordained by someone that doesn't even know you, then that is a major and serious problem. In order to be ordained, you must have been active in a local church under a ministry that is of God and effective.

For example, in Acts 19:11-17, God had done extraordinary things through Paul that even handkerchiefs and aprons that had touched him were taken to the sick and their illnesses were cured and the evil spirits left them. Some Jews who went around driving out evil spirits who were exorcists took upon them to call over them which had evil spirits using the name of the Lord Jesus saying, "In the name of Jesus, whom Paul preaches, I command you to come out." These men were the seven sons of Sceva, a Jewish chief priest.

One day, the evil spirit answered them and said, "Jesus I know, and Paul I know, but who are you?" Then the man who had the evil spirit jumped on them and beat them and sent them naked and bleeding and all the people were in fear and the name of the Lord was held in honor. The sons of Sceva were impressed with Paul's ability to drive out demons and heal the sick, but what they didn't realize was that it wasn't Paul doing it, but it was God and the Holy Spirit working through Paul. What these fellows didn't realize was that Paul was anointed and called by God to do this. My point is that just because you see an anointed preacher casting out devils, preaching and healing the sick by the Holy Spirit, doesn't mean you can do it. God has to call you to do those things.

Everybody isn't called to preach. Everybody is not anointed to cast out demons. Just be who God has called you to be and don't try and be like no one but yourself. If there is a call on your life to ministry, you don't have to rush the process and go online to people you don't know to give you a piece of paper saying you are ordained. Doing that makes you an illegal preacher or minister in the pulpit that will have to answer to God one day; just do it God's way and go through the proper process to be the man or woman that God has called you to be. Don't be illegal in the ministry because it isn't worth it. A title is just a title. The title doesn't make you. There are so many people with titles, but they have no anointing. There are people that have titles who aren't anointed. There are people with no titles who are anointed.

It is time for you to come out of the tomb, but make sure you come out of the tomb right and with your spiritual weapons armed and ready for battle. The devil knows who is anointed and who isn't. If you are an illegal minister who is trying to battle demons and do ministry when you haven't truly been ordained, then the devil will tear you up like he did the seven sons of Sceva. They thought they could do what Paul did in Acts 19:11-17, but Paul had a relationship with God. Paul had been in the tombs of life and now he came out of the tomb with power and anointing. God called Paul to the ministry. God called Paul to preach and teach. God called Paul to heal the sick and to cast out devils. What you must realize is that God does the calling, you don't. Let God place you in the ministry that he has called you to be in. The enemy has placed himself as a guard at your tomb and the enemy has you not only locked up in your tomb, but he has you sealed in your tomb. The reason why God has permitted you to be locked up in your tomb of your trial is so you can go to the next dimension in your relationship with the Lord.

Job, for example, was definitely under attack by the enemy. Metaphorically speaking, he had a tomb experience, but God permitted him to be attacked just to show the devil that Job would serve him under any condition. Some of you are in your own tomb of life right now, but God is saying, "Count it all joy while you are in your tomb." It is just a matter of time before God is going to bring you out of your tomb. You may be in your tomb locked up and being tempted while you are in your tomb, but count it all joy. You may have some things that you need worked out at a certain time, but count it all joy. Your finances may not be where you want them to be, but count it all joy. Tombs are a part of life. God uses the tombs of life to put you in a place of maturity in him. Paul puts it like this: "When I was a child, I spake as a child, I understood as a child, I thought as a child: but when I became a man, I put away childish things." (1Corithians 13:11) Now that you are no longer a child in Christ, you should know what to do and what not to do. For those of you who are not believers, this is your chance to come out of the tomb of the world and give your life to Jesus Christ, so you can be all that God has called you to be in him.

The chief priests and Pharisees sent guards to the tomb and had it sealed because they said that the disciples could come and steal the body and say he had risen. They said it would be a worse deception than the first. This meant that if the disciples were to say Jesus had risen, then it would be worse than him saying he was the Son of

God when he was alive. Some of you have been sealed in the tombs of life and the enemy has sealed you in your tomb and you don't know how you are coming out. You are stuck in your tomb because there have been guards posted at your tomb, but count it all joy. You are about to be exposed to the God that is really in you. Let the enemy think you are defeated and that you won't make it; when you go into the tomb like you are defeated, you have to come out of the tomb with the victory. To be dead in Christ Jesus means that you are a new creature and that you no longer live by the governing of your flesh, but you are now being governed by the Spirit of God, which is the Holy Spirit. Go ahead in your tomb because you are about to come out of the tomb alive in Jesus Christ. Once you come out of the tomb, then you can rest. "On the seventh day God…rested." (Genesis 2:2) The Hebrew word for rested is shabath, which means eternally or heavenly rest. It was not that God was tired. God is spirit, which in Hebrew means ruach, which means wind, or breath. God's work was complete and he could rest from his work that he had done to create the universe.

You can also experience the Greek word called chrisma, which means endowment or chrism, which is of the Holy Spirit. The Greek word endowment means to furnish with something freely or naturally. The Greek for chrisma is the anointing or unction. There was a violent earthquake from heaven and the stone was rolled back from the tomb. Jesus' appearance was like lightning and his clothes were white as snow. White represents purity. You have been through long enough and you have a pure God that wants you out of the tomb. You have a pure God that wants you saved and set free. You have a pure God that wants you to realize what your purpose and destiny is on this earth. You have been through the storms of life and now it is your season to walk into what God has called you to do. For you unbelievers, it is time for you to make a change for the better. Tomorrow is not promised. God is calling you to stir up your gift that he gave you before the foundations of the earth. You may or may not realize it, but God has gifted you with a ministry. You have a gift that God has given you, but it is up to you to seek God and find out what your gift is so you can be effective on this earth for the kingdom of God.

In 2Timothty, Paul talks about Timothy's mother and grandmother and says to stir up the gift of God that God has already placed in him. Timothy's mother and grandmother were early Christian converts, possibly through Paul's ministry. Timothy was encouraged by Paul to persevere and use spiritual gifts in the ministry. At the time of Timothy's ordination, he received special gifts to serve in the church and his anointing went to another dimension in God.

Once you come out of the tomb, it is time to stir up the gifts that God has given you. You may not think you are gifted or have destiny or purpose, but I encourage you and tell you that you are gifted and you have a wonderful future ahead of you, if you keep God first and seek after the face of God. The devil should have killed you while he had the chance because now you are reading this book and if you apply it to your life your life will never be the same again. When the enemy sealed you in a tomb, he thought you were going to stay dead. Now you are about to bust up out of the tomb right up in the devil's face. For the unbelievers, you are about to bust out of the tomb into salvation and get saved. It is not how you go into the tomb that determines your anointing in Christ, but it is how you bust out of the tomb that determines who you are in Christ.

On the third day, death could no longer hold Jesus anymore. I don't know when your third day experience will come, but when your third day experience comes, then no devil or enemy can stop what God is about to do in your life, if you just have faith and believe that God can bring you out of the tombs of your life. God has positioned you in a place where the tomb you were once in can no longer hold you any longer. The reality is that you have outgrown your tomb. I don't care what you are going through, you are still blessed. It doesn't matter what people say or think about you, you are still blessed. I don't care what happened recently or in your past, you are still blessed. It doesn't matter what your marriage, your finances, or your children are looking like, you are still blessed and you still have the victory. Jesus Christ did not die for you to be defeated; he died so you could have the victory over the powers of the enemy. Get, get, get, get on up out of that tomb!! Get your deliverance. Get your job. Get your finances. Get your marriage. Get your rebellious children. Just reach out and grab it!!! Leap out of the tomb. Leap out of your problems. Leap out of that sex out of marriage. Leap out of that immoral life style. Leap off of that alcohol and drugs. Leap out of that gambling. Leap out of that ungodly relationship. I encourage you and let you know that you can and will make it. It is time for you to come out of the tomb. It is time for you to come out of the tomb with power and anointing from on high.

CHAPTER EIGHTEEN

YOUR HATERS ARE SETTING YOU UP

– 1Samuel 18:1-16 –

What do you do when the very person that appears to be for you tries to sabotage your destiny? What I have realized is that we all have a destiny and this type of world we are living in today is the type of world where everyone wants to do something great in this life. People aspire to be successful. There is nothing wrong with wanting to be successful in life, but when your success takes you away from God, you have made your success an idol. When you are trying to be successful without having Jesus Christ first in your life, you are not truly successful in God's eyes. We are living in a world where people have their own free will and so many people today think that they are the lord of their lives. You are not the lord of your life; Jesus Christ is the Lord over your life. Your life does not belong to you, but it belongs to God. There is a higher power and there is a God. One day you will have to give an account for the way you lived your life on this earth and you will also give an account of the decisions you made while living on this earth.

In 1Samuel 18, we see jealousy, bitterness, resentment, indignation and all of these negative attributes in one man by the name of Saul, who was made king over Israel. You must understand that Samuel was a judge for Israel with a very powerful prophetic anointing on his life. Samuel had appointed his sons to be judges over Israel, but they turned out to be corrupt. In 1Samuel 8, Israel asked for a king. The reasons for this could have been because Samuel's sons were not godly enough to lead Israel and because the 12 tribes of Israel continually had problems working together; each tribe had its own leader and territory. One of the problems in churches today is that they want to do things their way instead of God's way. God is calling the church to be on one accord. It is hard to be on one accord in the body of Christ when rebellion is in the camp. It is hard to be on one accord in the body of Christ when pastors and preachers are jealous of other pastors and preachers. We should be on one accord. Saul appeared to be godly, but he was religious and not committed. Another reason they wanted a king was because they wanted to be like the other nations. God definitely didn't want that. God didn't mind them having a king, but he wanted them to have a king for the right motives. When someone wants to connect with you, you must ask yourself what their motives are for wanting to connect with you. For example, whenever someone wants to date you or draw closer to you, you need to wonder if they have a positive motive or negative motives.

The Israelites came out of Egypt by the hand of God through Moses, but they got very corrupt and didn't want God anymore. Theologically speaking, these were God's people; these were the people that God had chosen, but later on they rejected God and went away from the Lord. So many people in the church are there for the wrong reasons. There are some people in the church who are there, but they are not seeking that closer relationship with God. God is calling his people into holiness. "Be holy, for I am holy." (Leviticus 11:45) If God is telling you to be holy because he is holy, then that means it is possible to live a holy life. God will never ask you to do something that you can't accomplish. Your heart needs to be sanctified by God. Once your heart is changed, it will make it much easier for you to love more and even love your enemies. Saul could never tell the truth and was very indignant and full of pride. The way you can tell that you are full of pride is when you make a mistake and won't admit that you made a mistake and you were wrong; you know you have issues that you are struggling with and you hide behind them. It is only a trick of the devil to make you not admit your issues to yourself and to God and it will keep you in bondage. It doesn't matter how anointed and holy you are, you will still make mistakes. Some of the most anointed people have made major mistakes in life.

Abraham, who had the gift of faith and was made the father of many nations, made mistakes. He lied about his wife Sarah being his sister when she was his wife, but God still used him mightily. God said that all nations will be blessed through Abraham. (Genesis 18:18) In order to overcome your issues, you need to admit your mistakes to yourself and always make sure you learn from your issues and mistakes. Mistakes only create opportunities for success. The mistakes of yesterday are a stepping stone to your destiny. If you won't admit to and take responsibility for your mistakes, it only cripples your future and will cause rebellion and pride to creep in. Samuel anointed Saul as king, but Saul was indignant, envious, and jealous and could never tell the whole truth. God still told Samuel that this was the man he wanted anointed as king of Israel. (1Samuel 9:1-17) I believe that God is willing, just, and sovereign and he will give you a chance. In Samuel 15, the Lord rejects Saul as king because of his lifestyle. When I say reject, I am not saying that God gave up on Saul, but I am saying that God rejected him leading the Israelites because of his ungodly behavior. He says, "Rebellion is as the sin of witchcraft, and stubbornness is as iniquity and idolatry." (1Samuel 15:23)

In today's world, the people that are stubborn and who are idolaters usually are the ones who are rebellious and full of pride and you can't tell them anything. David defeated Goliath who was nine feet tall. Little old David defeated him with a bag with a stone in it. (1Samuel 17) They wanted to dress David up like a soldier with a sword and David said, "I don't need all of that because I have God." God is calling you to use the sword of the Spirit, which is the Word of God. You cannot be in the flesh using the Word of God. David cut off Goliath's head with his own sword. After this matter, Saul wanted to know who David was and David had Goliath's head in his hand while talking to Saul. You must realize that you are going to defeat the enemy with your sword; you are going to cut the enemy's head off in the spirit. It may seem like your haters and your enemies are getting the best of you. It may seem like your job is getting the best of you. It may seem like you are having so many difficulties in life, but there are better days ahead for you. Your enemies and your haters are only setting you up to be blessed of the Lord. The best way to defeat your enemies is to be successful. Even some of your own family members can be jealous and indignant of your success.

Saul was raging full of jealousy and envy towards David. (1Samuel 18) Even though Saul was jealous of David, he still had to bless him. Saul had no clue of who David was in the beginning. That is how it is for some of you; your haters are jealous of you and not respecting you for who you are. You must not worry; by them mistreating you, they are only pushing you into greatness in God. I can boldly state that because so many people put me down and said I would never make it and gave up on me. It only made me seek after God and made me want to succeed in God the more. There were a lot of people that were saying I had been in college for so long and they thought I would never graduate, but the Lord blessed me to graduate. Back in the beginning of this book, I talked about what I went through spiritually and God still blessed me to be able to graduate; and I was a double major, now that is God. Your haters are only setting you up to be blessed. You should thank God that you got hurt. You have been thinking that this thing or person was for you, so God had to allow you to be misunderstood just so you can depend totally on him. Jonathan became one in spirit with David, meaning they became best friends and he loved him as himself. Jonathan was Saul's son. He was a man of God, he respected David and he knew that David would be the next king. You can really learn something from that. What you can learn is that Jonathan was not stuck on titles or having power over people; he wanted to be in God's will and he knew it wasn't God's will for him to be the next king. Jonathan didn't want to place himself in a position that God didn't call him to. Jonathan and David became best friends and Jonathan made sure that he was not consumed by his father, Saul. I believe that God places people in your life that don't want to see you get consumed by the enemy. Jonathan made a covenant with David because he loved him as himself.

When you love yourself, it will be easy for you to love other people and it will also be easy for you to love your enemies and the people who have hurt you the most in life. Jonathan took off the robe he was wearing and gave it to David. They based their friendship on their commitment to God. God is calling us to base our friendships on our commitment to God and not on whether or not they can do something for you or if you can do something for them. You cannot buy love; true love is not something you can purchase. You cannot make people love you; they have to do that willingly.

Jonathan and David's friendship was based on their love for God. Being that they loved God, it was easy for them to get along and love each other. You must have pure motives on why you do things for people, like David and Jonathan. I have a friend named Robert Beasley and when I met him he was so nice. I got to know him more and more and I realized that he had a genuine heart and he just blesses me beyond measure. I feel like I have known him for years. He just loves to give to me and bless me and he never asks for anything in return. Our friendship is pure and based on positive motives. He is a great man who loves to be a blessing to me and I love him for that. Those are the kind of friends that people need. I have another friend named Regina Ferguson and she is CEO of a major corporation. I met her through my wife and she has always been a blessing to me and my wife. She is always blessing us and giving to us and she asks for nothing in return. Yet, she is always giving and being a blessing to people and I love her for that. Robert and Regina are my David and Jonathan because they bless from the heart and are not looking for anything in return. David and Jonathan's friendship was tested on several occasions. Jonathan could have easily had David killed, but he chose to love David and respected the fact that David was chosen to be the next king over Israel. Whatever Saul sent David to do, he did it with success. Saul gave him a high rank in the army and God was using that to prepare him for king.

God has called you for greatness, but you must be trained and prepared before God places you into your destiny. Even though Saul hated on David, he still had to bless him. Even though people are hating on you, they are only setting you up to be successful in who God has called you to be. You may not understand why you are going through what you are going through, but I am here to declare to you that you have to go through to get to. You may not understand why people treat you the way they treat you and you don't understand why you go through problem after problem, but God is setting you up for greatness. God uses the trials of life to shape your character and to shape you to be more like him. God has created you in his image and in his likeness. (Genesis 1:26) There are times you may have to endure some things; there are times where you just have to go through things in life, but God is setting you up for blessings. The very person you loved the most who ended up hurting you and walking out on you, what they didn't realize was that they only made you stronger. When you were with them, you felt like you couldn't live without them, but when God allowed them to go out of your life you then realized how strong you were the whole time. In that hurt, you realized that you can make it without that person that hurt you.

David was a little shepherd boy and he was being set up for greatness, but there were some things he had to go through and endure before he was positioned to his destiny, which was to be king over Israel. David was faced with death many times, but God had him shielded and protected. I am sure you have faced death plenty of times, but it was the hand of God that kept you away from death each time. Many of you have fallen in love with people that you thought you would spend the rest of your life with, only to realize that it wasn't going to happen. Now the one you loved the most has let you down. You must know and understand that you shouldn't put more of your trust in people than you do God. Man and woman will let you down, but God will never let you down. Many of you have made decisions that caused you to ask yourself how in the world you got in this situation. Now you wish you would have never done that, but God is a forgiving God and everyone makes mistakes. Your haters are setting you up to be great in God. Your mistakes are setting you up to be blessed by God. Your past is setting you up to be great. Don't let what you have done in the past or even what you have done recently cause you to give up or not try God. In situations like that is when you need to draw closer to God.

David was exalted in the army and everyone was pleased with him. Even in that, you realize that David had favor with God and man. Every person in the Bible that God used mightily had favor with God. Women came out from all the towns of Israel and said Saul had slain his thousands and David his tens of thousands. At that moment, Saul was very angry and got very jealous, In this world today, a great example would be a pastor telling another pastor that 20 people joined his church and the other pastor had no members to join. That could cause that pastor to get jealous and get the spirit of Saul. It shouldn't matter how many people join a pastor's church; what should matter is that people are coming to Jesus Christ, no matter what pastor God uses to do it through. We all serve the same God. I encourage you to not be jealous of other people because of their successes in life. The same God that blessed them is the same God that can bless you. God has no favorite people; he loves us all equal and the same. People who are jealous don't know who they are in Christ and they don't recognize the potential that God has given them. You have to be in the position of where God wants you to be and not man. You must rely on God to position you and not man. If you are uncertain of what your purpose is, then you need to pray and seek God. Trust that God will reveal it to you in due time.

God revealed my destiny to me when I gave my life to him. I wanted to play basketball, but God called me to preach, to pastor, to travel as an evangelist, and to be a Christian author. Had I not realized that, then I would have missed out on my destiny. If you have people in your life that are jealous of you, then show them love and be cautious at the same time. People who are jealous will try to do things secretly to hinder you from being who God has called you to be. If you are one that is jealous of someone's success, then you should ask God to help you not be jealous. The same God that blessed them is the same God that can bless you as well. If you are jealous, you must know it is not of God. You should ask God what your purpose is on this earth so you can be who God has called you to be. Being jealous of other people will only hinder your blessings and hinder what God wants to do in your life. The same God that blessed the person you are jealous of is the same God that can bless you as well. God has no favorite person; he loves us all the same and he wants to bless you as well.

CHAPTER NINETEEN

TAKE THE LIMITS OFF OF ME AND RELEASE ME

– Matthew 14:22-33 –

What do you do when you are in the ship of your situation and you are in the sea of your problem? It may seem like the sea is getting the best of you. You want to be free, but you don't know how. You are in a comfort zone of your flesh and you are thinking that everything is okay, but in God's eyes it is not okay. Being that you have been walking in the flesh so long, you don't even know what it is like to walk in the spirit; you are spiritually crippled. You are in a comfort zone and you have been limited by the sea of life. Life situations have got you down; the things that happened in your life have you depressed and you don't even know how you are going to come out. There are things that have happened and some things that are going on in your life that make you wonder if God is really with you. God is there and he sees all and knows all. When the enemy throws his life situations your way, you can tell the devil that he is already defeated by the blood of Jesus. You don't have to be a Bible scholar or a Bible genius to rebuke the devil. Demons tremble at the name of Jesus. Just say, "In the Name of Jesus, satan I rebuke you." Speak it with authority; speak it with power and authority in Jesus name!!

You may have been limited by the storms that have happened to you in life, but when all else fails, you have Jesus to fall back on. When you study the life of Christ, you will find that when he did miracles and healings, he was always moved with compassion. When I say compassion, I mean he was merciful for his people and he had a driving point in him to bring people out of bondage. His main goal for being on this corruptible earth was to redeem man and to bring man into relationship with him. In this story, you have the incarnate Christ, who was God in bodily form, who had descended (meaning came down) to miraculously demonstrate his divinity and deity. In this story, Christ proves that he is full of the Holy Ghost. Without the Holy Ghost and direction from his Father, he would not have done what he was given permission to do. I have discovered that a lot of people rely on the world. God is calling people to rely on him and him only. Jesus constrained his disciples to get into the ship. The Greek word for constrained is anagkazo, which means to make necessary or important. When Christ commanded them to do this, he meant that it was important because he needed time alone where he could pray and seek the face of God.

There are times where you just need to be alone with God and get in his presence and find out the will of God for your life. You need the power of the Holy Ghost in your life, so when you start going through in life you will be able to handle any situation that you come up against. God wants to take the limits off you and he wants to release you into greatness, but you can't be released into greatness if you have limits on you. Man will put limits on you, but God will take the limits off of you and allow you to be all you can be in him and in him alone. Jesus sent the multitude away so he could spend time with himself and God. I can tell you by experience, when you spend time alone with God and seek his face, it will really increase your anointing and make you stronger spiritually. When you get into the presence of God for real – I am not talking about when you go to church – but when you spend that quiet one-on-one time with God, something will happen and your life will never be the same. Once you have a divine encounter with God, you will never be the same again. Sometimes we want to be quick to blame everything on other people, but the real enemy is ourselves. Have you ever noticed some people always attract the wrong kind of people and they keep getting hurt by different people? If you renew your mind with the Word of God and change your life and change the way you think, then you will begin to attract the right kind of people. One thing I have realized is that the closer I get to God, the more I realize I really need him.

Jesus sent them away and he went up into a mountain apart to pray. When evening came, he was there alone. Sometimes you have to be willing to be alone. I have realized that we are living in a time where no one wants to be alone. Once you start being alone, you then have to face who you really are and so many people don't want to face who they really are. More anointing from God comes when you spend time alone with God. Jesus Christ spent time alone with God to pray so he could stay empowered to do the work that God had called him to do. There is power when you pray; there is more anointing when you pray; there are more blessings when you pray. The word pray in the Greek is proseuchomai, which means to God to supplicate, which means beg, to ask earnestly, or plead for help. Theologically speaking, I can imagine Jesus Christ was asking God to strengthen him, lead him and guide him. When are you going to ask God to lead and guide your life? Have you actually made Jesus

Christ your Lord and Savior? Does Christ really have total control of your life?

The ship was now in the midst of the sea, tossed with waves. Some of you right now are in the midst of the sea, tossed by the waves of your problems and situations. Many of you are carrying many different waves of problems in your life and you may have the sea of unforgiveness, the sea of doubt, the sea of fear, the sea of jealousy, or the sea of bitterness and hatred towards people, but I tell you that God can bring you out of it. He wants to take the limits off of you and release you into greatness. All you have to do is step out on faith and walk on water towards Jesus, like Peter did. "In the fourth watch of the night Jesus went unto them, walking on the sea." (Matthew 14:25) This was proof of Jesus' deity and of him being the Son of the Living God; being God in the flesh at this time. No ordinary man could walk on water unless Jesus allowed him to, like Jesus allowed Peter, to teach Peter to keep his eyes on him. Are you ready to walk on the water of your promise? Are you ready for God to take the limits off of you and release you? God is calling you to take up your cross and follow him and deny and humble yourself. How do you take up your cross and follow after Christ? You have to realize that you are in need of a Savior, who is Jesus. You must know that Jesus is the answer to your problems. You must know that you are a sinner in need of Jesus. There are some sacrifices you have to make in order for you to live for Jesus Christ. When you sacrifice your life of sin for Jesus Christ, you will not only receive blessings, but you will receive eternal life in heaven. When God is taking the limits off of you and releasing you into greatness, you cannot want to be in the world and live for God at the same time. You have to want to surrender everything for the sake of Jesus Christ. Jesus told them to get in the ship and go on ahead of him. He gave them orders. God is calling us to do the work of the ministry and to live a holy life. While you have things that you will do for him now, you cannot let the storms of life and life situations distract you from being who God has called you to be.

The disciples saw Jesus walking on the water and they were troubled. They thought it was a spirit and they cried out in fear. They were with Jesus for a while, sat under his teaching and saw his miracles, but still could not recognize him from a distance. You are destined for greatness and God just has you in hiding mode right now. He is preparing you for the ministry, business, or financial breakthrough that he has for you. It is just a matter of time before God releases you into your destiny. God is about to release you into greatness. All the people are going to wonder how in the world you got to your destiny, but you are going to say it was nothing but the

Lord that got you there. When God blesses you and places you into your destiny, make sure you give him the credit and give him the glory that he deserves. You have to be careful how you treat people because you don't know what they will become in the future. They might be the very one that blows up in success right in your face. God is about to take the limits off of you and he is about to reveal himself to you and the plan that he has for your life. In order for you to be released into your destiny, you must respond to God in obedience.

Jesus calms his disciples by saying, "Be of good cheer; it is I; be not afraid." (Matthew 14:27) That is what God is trying to tell you: "Be of good cheer; it is I; be not afraid." Jesus is saying to be of good cheer because he knows what you are going through. He knows you have been hurt; he knows that your heart needs to be healed; all of this is only a set up for the limits to be taken off of you for you to be released. Many of you have a call on your life to ministry. I am not saying you are all called to preach, but many of you reading will be preachers, pastors, evangelists and great people in the ministry; but you have to be willing to surrender your life to Christ. That is so important and essential for being an effective Christian; you have to be willing to let go of your worldly desires to seek to live a life of Christ. The sins you do and consistently fall short in can't give you permanent satisfaction like Jesus can; only Jesus can satisfy you permanently. All Jesus Christ wants is your heart. Once he gets your heart, it makes it easy for you to submit to him and surrender your life to him. Then it becomes easy for you to obey him in everything. The closer you get to Christ, the easier it will be to love people who are not so easy to love. The world loves people who love them, but the test comes when you can love people who don't love you and who have hurt you. That is what Jesus Christ did; Jesus loved people who didn't love him back. He forgave his own people for crucifying him.

Peter says, "Lord, if it be thou, bid me come unto thee on the water." (Matthew 14:28) At that moment, God was taking the limits off of Peter. When Peter got out there, he started to look at what was around him which was the winds, waves, sea and the storm, and he lost focus. All Peter had to do was to keep his eyes on Jesus when he was out on the water and he would have made it to Jesus. I challenge you to hold God to his Word; he will always respond to his Word and back up his Word because he is the Word. Tell the Lord and say, "Lord, if you exist, then please show me or reveal yourself to me." I guarantee God will show you who he is.

Jesus told Peter to come and walk on water with him. Because Peter heard his Savior's voice, he responded in obedience to his

Savior. You have to be willing to walk on water with Jesus. What I mean by that is having faith in God in any and every kind of circumstance that you come up against. Walk on water with your faith; when you are sick in your body, exercise the gift of faith. You cannot walk with Jesus for a little while and then when the devil begins to attack, you start to get flaky in your walk with God. When the storms of life come and bad times start to occur, if you start to take your eyes off of Jesus in the midst of your situations, then you will begin to sink in your issues, just like Peter did. "When he saw the wind boisterous, he was afraid." (Matthew 14:30) The Greek word for boisterous is ischuros, which means mighty, powerful and strong. Some of you have been going through a mighty, forcible and strong situation and you don't know how you are going to come out. You don't even see how you got in it. Some of you have lost some things, but God is saying that if you give your life to him and stay faithful during your boisterous storm, in due season, you will reap the harvest of blessings if you faint not. You have been waiting on your destiny for years and it seems like it isn't ever going to come to pass, but God is about to take the limits off of you and release you. Sometimes it seems like God is nowhere to be found, but even when God seems like he isn't there, then that is really when he is there.

What happened to Peter was he began to sink simply because he lost the faith. He had enough of faith to step out of the ship, but he didn't have enough faith to walk all the way to Jesus. Some people have enough faith to come to church on Sundays, some have enough faith to go to the altar when the preacher makes an altar call, but when it comes to you giving your life to Christ and letting go of that sinful lifestyle, then that is when people start to sink. They think, "I went to church, I went to Bible study, I pray at home, so that is enough." Some think they don't have to go to church to be saved or they don't have to read the Bible every day. When you start to have that kind of mindset that is when you start to sink for sure. The Bible says that Peter started to sink. One of the many reasons why he started to sink was because he didn't have enough faith to keep walking towards Jesus.

When you have faith in Jesus Christ in the midst of a storm, as long as you keep your eyes on him, then you will not sink at all. Some of you are sinking now in your situations simply because there is no connection with God, God is calling you right now to connect with him. If you are an unbeliever, you can connect with him today. If you have fallen away from God, you can reconnect with him right now. The gift of salvation is a free gift. Once you receive the gift of salvation, you have access to whatever it is that God has to offer you. Once you give your life to Jesus Christ, you have access to deliverance, joy, peace, prosperity, good health, heaven or eternal life, and healing. This is what salvation has to offer you and there is no other way you can receive salvation without going through Jesus Christ. You receive salvation through Jesus and Jesus only. The only way you can get to God is through Jesus. There is no other way to be saved accept through Jesus Christ. You may even be in church, but there still can possibly be a disconnection between you and God. God is seeking to take the limits off of you and release you. You must know and understand that God has a plan for your life. You may not know what your purpose is on this earth is right now, but God knows. If you get connected with God, then he will slowly reveal or show you your purpose for being on this earth. You may not think you are gifted because of what you went through in your past, but you are gifted, you are special, and you are blessed. It doesn't matter how you were raised, you still can be successful. You may have not had your father with you when you were growing up or your family didn't show you love, but you still can be a success in God. God wants to release you into your promise and he also wants to release you out of your bondage, but you must step out on faith and try him. You have tried everything else; why not try a God that loves you? You must first know and understand that God loves you and he wants you to be saved. You must first repent and then give your life to him. (Romans 10:9)

Jesus says, "O thou of little faith, wherefore didst thou doubt?" (Matthew 14:31) Peter had enough faith to step out because he knew his Savior's voice, but his faith was not consistent. If his faith was consistent, then he would have made it to Jesus when he stepped out of the boat. When Jesus got into the boat, the storm ceased. You may be going through a bad situation and it seems like the devil has been getting the best of you, but the devil is only coming against you because of the anointing and call that is on your life. God is taking you out of your comfort zone so you can do the work which he has given you to do. Storms come, tornadoes come, hurricanes come; but at some point and time, they have to go away; they have to cease. God is about to take the limits off of you and release you.

I want everyone to know that I love you so much in Christ. The Lord wants to use you. No matter what you have done, you still can be a success. I want you to know that you are not a failure. You may have made some bad decisions, but God still loves you. I believe in you. I know you can achieve anything in life. I know you can make it. Do you believe you can make it? You must believe it for yourself. God blesses those who respond to him in faith. I know a man that while he was on earth was limited to time and space; he was lied on, talked about, abused, misunderstood, falsely accused, accused of blasphemy and was limited to time and space. He was beaten all night long, his flesh began to come off of his body, he had crowns of thorns put on his head, and he died on an old rugged cross. He was without sin and was perfect while being on earth. Now he sits at the right hand of the Father, who is in heaven. This man is interceding on our behalf to his Father. This man I am talking about is Jesus Christ, the Messiah, the Anointed One. The limits have been taken off of him and he has been released. This same Jesus is a man you can have a personal relationship with. He knows everything about you. Jesus can take away those bad habits you possess; he can take you out of that immoral lifestyle if you allow him to. "They that were in the ship came and worshiped him, saying, Of a truth thou art the Son of God." (Matthew 14:33) That is all Jesus Christ wants you to do; worship him, believe in him and accept him as your personal Lord and Savior. Sometimes God will allow you to sink in life so you can realize you are weak and that you are in need of a Savior, who is Jesus Christ. You can make it, but the only way you can make it is to have Jesus Christ first in your life. The Lord loves you, which is why he sacrificed his life for you. God is waiting for you and he is ready to take the limits off of you. He wants to release you into that place he has ordained you to be.

CHAPTER TWENTY

YOU'VE COME TOO FAR TO TURN BACK NOW

– Mark 14:32-42 –

Have you ever looked back on your life and everything you have ever been through and said to yourself, "Look at where God has brought me from"? Have you ever observed your life and said, "God has brought me from a mighty long way"? The truth of the matter is that some of you have been through things that should have killed you, but because God has an awesome plan for your life and because of the grace and mercy of God, you are still here. There are things you may have gone through in life and, although you didn't realize how you came out of it at that time, it was the hand of God that pulled you out of the pit of darkness. The reason why you are still here is because God has a greater plan for your life.

There are some people that could not have survived what you went through; you are a living testimony. You must know and understand that the devil does not want you in relationship with God. He will use the cares of this world and life's obstacles and people to keep you from developing a relationship with Jesus Christ.

One thing I have discovered is that when you start seeking to live a holy life and be holy in the presence of God, satan really gets agitated. He doesn't mind you discussing holiness; he doesn't mind you talking about integrity and living a life that is pleasing in God's sight; but when you start living a holy life, then you become a major target to the enemy. Have you ever noticed that when you were not a Christian or not saved, it seemed like everything went okay and that you didn't have many problems; but the moment you gave your life to Jesus Christ, then it seems like all odds were against you and you started having problem after problem. The reason why you started having so much difficulty is because you are saved now and the devil doesn't like that. He figures if he attacks you, then you will turn your back on God. You must know that anytime you become a believer the devil will throw his fiery darts at you and he will try to do everything he can to distract you. The devil messes with people who are gifted and anointed by God and who have great destiny and purpose. The enemy isn't worried about the people who are not saved and who are living for him; he already has them. Now that you are saved, he is after your soul and he wants you back with him. The devil has gotten a glimpse of your future and where God is about to take you in the Spirit and ministry. He is going to do everything he can to keep you from fulfilling the call and purpose God has on your life.

Jesus Christ is at end of his earthly ministry; Peter had already denied him and the councils of religious leaders had already condemned him. Ask yourself this question. It isn't to judge you or to make you feel bad, but it is to make you think and do a self check. For the ones that are saved, how many times have you denied Jesus Christ since you have been saved? If the world would condemn you for believing in Jesus Christ, would you still serve him and stick with him until your time is up on this earth? Look at how God has still extended his grace, his love and his mercy towards you. In this element of scripture, Jesus is at Gethsemane and he tells his disciples to sit here while he prays. This was a place where he often went to pray and to be alone with his Father, who is known as God. Being alone with God is an awesome thing. We take the time out to be alone with people we love; we take time to be intimate with our spouses or if you are dating a person you want to always spend time with that person you are dating because you want to know all about them. That is what God wants. He wants that alone time with you; he wants you to take time out of your busy schedule for you to get to know him. It's not that he doesn't know you; he knows everything about you because he created you, but he wants you to get to know him. When you are alone with and seeking the face of God, that is when you receive instruction, wisdom, power from the Holy Ghost and knowledge from on high.

Jesus spent a lot of time in prayer during his earthly ministry, which was why he was so successful. If you study the life of Jesus Christ, you will find that Jesus didn't reach a lot of people like his disciples did. Jesus planted a seed in them that was watered by the Holy Ghost. Jesus was in agony at Gethsemane and this was a place where he was really challenged. Even God in the flesh came to a point in his life that he thought about all that he had went through on this earth the 30 some years he was on this earth. He knew what he came to the earth to do, but when that time came, he was in agony and stressed about it. I must tell you that what Jesus faced was a physical death; if Jesus faced death, we will have to face death as well. When you are in sin and doing things that God doesn't like, you don't think about physical death because the devil has you so caught up in the sin. You came into this world and you are going to die one day. That is just a part of life and that isn't something you can escape. I don't care how rich you are or how much power you have on earth, you will still have to die. Even the President of the United States of America has to die. Even though they were the President of the United States, if they were not saved, then they still won't make it into heaven. What you are on earth won't get you into heaven. The only thing that can get you into heaven is being a Christian and living a life that is pleasing to God.

I know for me, when I first gave my life to Jesus Christ, I thought all my troubles would go away. As I began to mature in God, I realized that in this world you will have troubles and I would be persecuted. When I was in college, they called me a Bible boy, but I don't regret it at all because God has kept me and blessed me so much. When Jesus was in ministry when he was on earth, he endured heavy persecution by his own people, by Pharisees, and by religious leaders. They treated him so badly and they didn't understand his teaching because his teaching came from his Father. Now he is at the climax of his ministry; the highest point of his ministry and that is to be crucified on an old rugged cross for the world's sins. This was a point where he was going to be separated from the God Almighty. Many of you are being faithful to God, you come to church, you come to Bible study and it seems like nothing is still working out for you. Just keep the faith and persevere in your walk with God because you may be being tested by God. God allows things to happen in our lives to motivate us to seek him and draw closer to him. One thing I have realized is that you cannot escape trouble; this world is not trouble free and there will always be something that you will have to go through as long as you are living. Can you serve God with no money in the bank? Can you serve God with no job? Can you serve God when a loved one dies or if you lose everything you have?

Jesus took Peter, James and John with him and he began to be deeply distressed and troubled. (Mark 14:33) You may wonder how, from a theological perspective, Jesus got distressed and troubled. You must understand that he was fully man, but because he was also fully God, he was still without sin because God cannot sin. He was distressed and troubled. Distressed means he was in pain, or suffering. He was in agony because he knew the horrendous death he was about to endure and he didn't like the fact that he would be separated from his Father when dying on the cross for the world's sin. I encourage you right now that when you feel like giving up on life and on God, start thinking about where God has brought you from and what Jesus went through on the cross just for you. Speak to yourself and encourage yourself and tell yourself that you have come too far to turn back now. When the devil attacks your husband, when he attacks your wife, your kids, your finances, your job, your health, or your mind, you should declare to yourself that God has brought you too far to turn back now. When life's obstacles begin to strike you in the head, say to yourself that you have come too far to turn back now. When doors start shutting in your face and it seems like no other doors are opening in your life, say to yourself that you have come too far to turn back now; keep on trying until another door opens. To be honest, God sometimes allows doors to be shut in your life just to protect you; he is an all knowing God and he can see things that you can't see.

Jesus' soul is overwhelmed with sorrow to the point of death. (Mark 14:34) This was a point in Jesus' life that he did not want to go through. He knew he would be in major agony and pain. Many of you have lived your life separated from God and you didn't even realize it. Right now God is calling you back into relationship with him. God is calling you to pray more and not just a five minute prayer. God is calling you to really seek his face and pray with a pure and sincere heart. God is calling you to take time out of your busy schedule to slowly develop a relationship with him. You may say you don't know God, but God knows you and he is waiting for you to get to know him.

Jesus was overwhelmed to the point of death and he felt like he couldn't do it, but he was strengthened. Some of you have gone through things in life and you didn't know how you were going to come out of it, but it is the hand of God that brought you out. If God brought you out of your past, then he is definitely a God that can deliver you again. How many of you right now are going through within yourself or know people who are going through within themselves? One thing I have realized is that sometimes your worst enemy can be yourself. The best way to defeat you is to face you. Jesus told his disciples to stay watch. Each time, he found his disciples getting weary and sleepy. How many times have you gotten weary and sleepy on God, but he still loved you? Jesus has already paid the price for our sins, he has given up the ghost for us and death no longer has a hold on you. Jesus says stay here and keep watch. He fell to the ground and prayed that if possible, the hour might pass from him. (Mark 14:35) In every situation in life that you have ever encountered, there is something to be learned. God knows everything that has ever happened in your life. He wants what you have gone through to be a learning experience. Nothing in your life happens without God first knowing about it. That is one thing you cannot do; trick God. He knows your heart and he knows the things you hide from man. For example, you may be hiding that you are jealous of someone else. That person that you are jealous of may not know it right then, but God knows it. The catch is, eventually the person will be able to pick up on it and see that you are jealous of them. You may trick man, but you cannot trick the Creator. God will test you and then he will reveal himself to you in the midst of the test. God tested Abraham to sacrifice his one and only son Isaac. When Abraham was about to sacrifice him, then God revealed himself to Abraham. (Genesis 22) The tests God takes you through are only to drive integrity out of you.

Sometimes before you start to operate in integrity, you have to know what it is like to not have integrity. For example, Peter told Jesus that he would stick with him no matter what. At that very moment Peter all the while thought he was a man of integrity and full of faith. Jesus says to Peter, "Before the cock crow twice, you shalt deny me thrice." (Mark 14:30) Peter had to be tested in that area so he could see his faults and so he could seek God for godliness and integrity. Peter obviously failed, but it didn't make him a failure.

Sometimes before you can operate in success, you have to first be familiar with failure. In order for you to be successful, you have to have had an appointment with failure. Many of you have been tested. If you haven't, then you must know and I warn you that you will be tested. You must know and realize that people are dying and going to hell every day. I pray that every unbeliever that will come in contact with this book will surrender and give their life to Christ. It is not enough to say you go to church or pray to God or do good things, but you must be saved and you must be born again and have given your life to Jesus Christ in order to make it into heaven. Going to church isn't good enough. You must do more than just go to church. You must go to church, get saved and then get active in church and in ministry. It is through confession from the mouth and the heart that salvation is given and salvation again is a free gift given by Jesus Christ our Lord and Savior. (Romans 10:9) You cannot do anything to earn salvation or to be saved; you just receive it as a gift from Jesus in him dying on the cross and offering it to you through and by love. Jesus showed his love for you by dying on a cross. He was without sin; he was perfect and never had done any wrong.

This book isn't designed to be deep. I want you to be able to see the simple message that I am seeking to give out to God's people. This book is very basic, but powerful and if applied it will change your life forever. We love Jesus because he first loved us. You cannot earn going to heaven by doing nice things for people. If you are not saved or born again and you do nice things, then that won't get you into heaven. You must get saved and live a righteous life in the sight of God in order to make it into heaven. Even as a preacher preaching, if the preacher lives an unholy life before God, but still preaches, he can't expect to make it into heaven. That isn't how God works. (Luke 13:22-28) You must be born again or saved to make it into heaven. (John 3:1-5) Jesus says, "Enter ye in at the strait gate: for wide is the gate, and broad is the way, that leadeth to destruction, and many there be which go in thereat: Because strait is the gate, and narrow is the way, which leadeth unto life, and few there be that find it." (Matthew 7:13-14) In other words, the gate that leads to heaven is narrow. That doesn't mean it is difficult to be saved, but it means that there is only one way to heaven and that is through Jesus and being saved. Only a few decide to really live for God. So many people want to live for the devil and live sinful lives. Living for God isn't popular, but in the end you will not regret giving your life to him. One thing you must know and understand is that you cannot say you are a believer and then live any kind of way you want; there has to be a sacrifice for Jesus. What this scripture is saying is that many people will go to eternal darkness which is hell, but few will go to heaven because so many people want to live for the devil. I encourage you to not be one of them that lives for the devil. Please make sure you get on that narrow path which is heaven.

Jesus says, "Abba, Father, all things are possible unto thee; take away this cup from me: nevertheless not what I will, but what thou wilt." (Mark 14:36) You can see that Jesus has surrendered his life and will over to his Father, who is God. That is what God wants you to do; surrender your life over to him completely. When you surrender your life completely over to God, it secures you and protects you from all of satan's traps. The best thing you can do in order for your house to be a house of the Lord is to pray and be an example. Let your family see the God in you. If you want them to change, then they first have to see the change in you. They need to see that God can change you and deliver you; then they will see that there is hope for them to change as well. Make sure that no matter what happens in your life that you don't give up on God. For the people who have never tried God, I encourage you to try him because your life will never again be the same if you try him. The world is not worth you turning your back on God.

Jesus "prayed that, if it were possible, the hour might pass from him." (Mark 14:35) He knew exactly what he was about to go through when he was on earth. The religious leaders tried so many times to catch Jesus in sin, but they could not. Being that he is all knowing, he knew exactly what was about to go down. Can you imagine having never sinned or done anything wrong and getting arrested for no reason? Jesus was arrested, he was ridiculed and they persecuted him for no reason at all. Not only was he beaten, but after he was beaten, he had to walk through the city with a very heavy wooden cross. He had to carry his cross after being beaten. That is what Jesus died for; so you can take all of your problems to the cross. What you must know and understand is that you cannot handle your problems, only God can. No matter what the problem or situation is, make sure you put it on the cross. You have come too far to turn back now. Jesus died for every problem that you have ever had and will have. He wants you to come to him when you are going through because Jesus is the problem solver. Take time out and look back over your life and where you are now; you will see that God was with you the whole entire time. Remember, you have come too far to turn back now.

CHAPTER TWENTY-ONE

YOU'RE TOO GIFTED TO BE DEFEATED

– 2Timothy 1:1-7 –

It is when you accept Jesus into your heart and receive the power of the Holy Ghost that you begin to realize that you have a gift from God. It is only through salvation and receiving the power of the Holy Ghost that God will begin to reveal to you just how gifted you really are. Salvation is being delivered from sin. It means to be rescued from sin. As you begin to mature and grow in the knowledge of God, you then will begin to realize you are gifted. After I gave my life to Christ and received the Holy Ghost, God started to deal with me about my call to ministry. Once I accepted the call to preach, he began to show me I was gifted to speak. When he showed me I was gifted to speak, I was so scared. I thought, "God, are you sure you are calling the right person to preach?" Then God showed me as I continued my walk with him that he had really called me to preach. I was always afraid of getting up in front of people to do public speaking, but thank God I accepted the call. Even today, I still get nervous when I have to preach.

The enemy doesn't want you to find out who you are as an individual in Christ. So many people don't know what their purpose for being on this earth is. They don't know what it is that God has created them to do. I have even discovered that people in the body of Christ don't know their mission in life. In order for you to know what God has called you to do on this earth for him, you really must seek his face and get to know him and then he will reveal it to you. A lot of people may think that they are just called to work a regular job and live from pay check to pay check, but God has so much more in store for you than just a regular job. God may be saying that he wants you to be a Christian entrepreneur and to establish and start your own business so you can do the work of the ministry. The truth of the matter is that you have a gift, whether you realize it or not. It is up to you to tap into the gift that God has given you to do on this earth. The main gift that God wants you to obtain is the free gift of salvation. Salvation is a gift that you can't earn. In order for you to make it into the kingdom, this is a gift you must have. You receive this free gift through total submission to God. This is the type of gift that transforms your mind or changes your mind for the better. (Romans 12:1-2)

One thing I have discovered is that some church people's minds have not been renewed and they allow the devil to keep them in defeat. There are so many Christians in this world that the enemy has walking in defeat and it shouldn't be that way. The enemy is trying to mess up the reputation of being a Christian. There are so many people in the church that are so gifted, but they just sit in the pew and allow their gift to go to waste. I must state that the gift does not define who you are, but it is your relationship with God that defines who you are. If the gift defines who you are or if it dictates who you are, then where would there be any room for God? You cannot rely on your gift to get you to your destiny; only God can get you to your destiny and keep you there. It takes more than just your gift to keep you in your future or your destiny; it takes having a relationship with God and integrity to keep you in your destiny. Many people rely on their gift, but God is not calling you to rely on your gifts. He is calling you to rely on him. He is the one who gave you the gift in the first place. One thing you must know is that God doesn't gift you to just to gift you so you can brag and say you are gifted. God gifts you so it can bring glory to him and be a blessing to his people. You must realize that when you are gifted, your gift will make room for you. When you are gifted, you don't have to force your way to the top. (Proverbs 18:16) People who are gifted are just gifted and they just roll with the flow of their gift. People who are not aware of their gift have to force their way in and they scheme their way to where they are trying to go in life. People who are conscious of their gift rely on the direction of the Holy Spirit to get them to their destiny in God.

Here in this passage of scripture, Paul is encouraging Timothy. Paul is saying that he is reminded of Timothy's sincere faith, which first lived in his grandmother Lois and in his mother Eunice. Paul is tells Timothy that he is persuaded that it now lives in Timothy as well. (2Timothy 1:5) I have realized that when you are gifted, other people will be able to recognize that you are gifted. Timothy was extremely gifted because he came from a lineage where his grandmother and mother were gifted in God. Gifted people don't have to try and be noticed because God will exalt them and God will raise them up. Timothy's grandmother Lois and his mother Eunice were early Christian converts, possibly through Paul's ministry in their home city. They obviously communicated their faith in God to Timothy, even though his father was probably not a believer. Timothy's gift was already in him from the beginning because God had placed it there, but it had to be stirred up. Paul encouraged Timothy to stir up the gift that was within him.

God is calling you to stir up your gift that is within you. One of the ways to stir up your gift is through faith. Faith is the key to unleashing your gift that is in you. You must rely on God for your gift to be stirred up. Another way to stir up your gift is to trust God. The Bible says, "Trust in the Lord with all thine heart; and lean not unto thine own understanding. In all thy ways acknowledge him, and he shall direct thy paths." (Proverbs 3:5-6) One thing I have realized is that it is hard to acknowledge God when you don't trust him. God has been taken out of the schools and we wonder why there is so much crime, alcohol, drugs, and sex in the schools; it is simply because God is not in the picture. On our money it says, "In God We Trust." If you really trust God and you say in God we trust, then why is God out of our schools? I have come to understand that it is only a trick of the enemy. You have gangs all over in the cities now. The reason why these young kids are going off in gangs is because they are not being properly raised by their parents. They are not getting enough attention and love. That is what a parent should do for their children is show them love and attention. The word 'acknowledge' means to recognize the rights or authority or to admit as true and to express thanks for. It is hard to acknowledge God in all your ways if you don't recognize his authority over you and the whole cosmos, which means universe. It's hard to acknowledge God when you have no respect for him and God's people. It's hard to acknowledge him when you don't admit he is true.

God is calling you to express your worship and love towards him. There may be a lot of things you have asked God for and it seems like it has been unanswered by God. You may have asked God things like, bless me with money, with a job, with a husband or a wife, with a car, with a house, Lord heal me, Lord deliver me. You must know that you have to bless God as well. Bless God in the way you treat other people. Make sure you are a tither and not robbing God. Make sure you are living an obedient life. All God asks for is a tenth of your income. Gifted people understand the concept of sowing seed. If you don't tithe, you are cursed with a curse. (Malachi 3:8-12) Gifted people don't rely on people to get them to their destiny. Gifted people rely on God and allow God to connect them with the people that can help them get to their destiny. People who are not conscious of their gift and don't understand who they are in God try to do things themselves and hook themselves up, rather than trusting and acknowledging God to place the people in their lives to help them. Gifted people trust in God and fleshly people trust in man. When you trust in man rather than in God, you will always get disappointed. Once you get disappointed, you will never be appointed. People who are gifted are always getting appointed, but the people who are not conscious of their gift are the ones who are getting disappointed and not appointed. The reason being is because they rely on their own intellect rather than relying on the intellect of God. That is why so many people get hurt in relationships; they didn't seek God to see if it was the right person for them because they were impatient. Being impatient can get you into a whole lot of trouble and can cause you to really get hurt. Gifted people say, "I may have been single for a while, but maybe God has me single because he is dealing with me and he is trying to pull stuff out of me and draw me closer to him." That is how a mature, gifted person would perceive it. You must be careful who you link up with today because a person can be the devil in disguise. It takes the discernment and the anointing of God for you to recognize the wolf in sheep's clothing.

You must understand that you are on your way somewhere. Are you on your way to the right place? You should put all of you confidence and trust in God because God will always lead you to the right place. God knows what is best for you. You must know and understand that you have a ministry and you cannot operate in ministry sitting down and not being who God has called you to be. God has called you to be a disciple of him. The word disciple means to learn or to spread the teachings of another. In order to teach or preach or minister the Word of God, you have to be taught. You cannot teach what you have not been taught. You cannot lead if you have never followed. You must get in God's Word and study it for yourself. You don't have to be a preacher to study God's Word. When you really think about it, we are all ministers of the Gospel. The word minister means to serve, so we are all called to be servants. I am not saying all people are called to preach and pastor, but we are all called to tell someone about Jesus, to serve God's people and to work in the ministry. Being a servant to God's people shows that you are meek and humble; having a teachable spirit shows that you are meek and humble. Gifted people are usually meek and humble and God can use those kinds of people mightily in the kingdom of God.

That is what Timothy was; Timothy was a humble servant and was mentored by the Apostle Paul. In this passage, Apostle Paul was encouraging Timothy to be faithful in his commitment to God and his call to ministry. The anointing was on Timothy's grandmother Lois and mother Eunice, which later transpired to Timothy. Timothy was a man that was very anointed and gifted. He was very humble and had a teachable spirit. The problem with some church people today is that they think they know everything and no one can tell them anything. It is in humility that you draw closer to God. You must know and understand that you can learn something from even the least of people. You can even learn something from an unbeliever. What made Jesus so anointed and effective in ministry was the fact that he submitted to his Father, who is in heaven. He submitted to God. If you learn to submit to God and then to leadership, it will get you a whole lot further in your relationship with God. The anointing comes from God. God uses the Holy Spirit to anoint and endow or empower. It takes the anointing for you to operate your gift. You cannot operate your gift without the anointing of God. It takes the anointing from God to stir up your gift from God. I don't care what you are going through in your life; allow God to stir up your gift that he has placed on the inside of you. You are too gifted to be defeated.

You may desire certain things from God, but God also desires certain things from you. Allow him to stir up what he has placed on the inside of you because you are too gifted to be defeated. Stir up your gift of obedience to God. When you stir up your gift of obedience to God, it releases God to bless you in so many ways. God has had mercy and grace on many of you and he has brought you out of situation after situation. Now it is time for you to walk into what God has in store for you. The Bible says that the Apostle Paul says to

Timothy to, "Stir up the gift of God, which is in thee by the putting on of my hands." (2Timothy 1:6) At the time of Timothy's ordination, he had received special gifts of the Spirit which enabled him to serve the church. If you have a gift, you need to utilize it or use it in the Body of Christ. The gift is not designed to make you powerful, but it is designed for you to bring glory to God and to bless God's people on this earth. The people who are gifted realize and understand that their gift that God has given them is to bring glory to God and to do damage to the devil's kingdom. The enemy has been attacking you in so many different ways and now it is time for you to fight back with your gifted self against the devil with your gift that God has given you. You must know that satan doesn't want you to realize you have a gift for the Body of Christ. Once you realize you have a gift for the Body of Christ, you start to realize who you are in Christ. You have been picked on by the devil long enough and now it is time for you to get a fight in your spirit and fight back in the Spirit of God. You have been walking in defeat long enough; it is time for you to put on the whole armor of God. It's time for you to put on the helmet of salvation, put on the breast plate of righteousness, put on the shield of faith and pull out your sword of the spirit, which is the Word of God. (Ephesians 6:14-17) Gifted people will put on the whole armor of God. Gifted people will fight the good fight of faith.

I understand it may be hard for you; you may be a single parent or may be going through some type of situation, but you must know and understand that you are too gifted to be defeated. Yes, I know you are called to the ministry and many of you are called to preach, teach, evangelize, pastor and serve in many capacities in the church and ministry, but you still must know that you are gifted. The devil is throwing everything he can at you already because he knows you are gifted and he doesn't want you to realize how anointed and how special you are to God. God knows what is best for his people and he knows what is best for you. He holds your future right in his hand. You may choose to go your way, but your way isn't near as good as his way. You can choose to go your way and not God's way, but it will not bring you satisfaction in the long run. It may seem satisfactory in the beginning, but it won't last long at all.

It seems like the enemy is throwing everything at you at one time to keep you weak in the flesh, but by now in this book you should be aware of the tactics of the devil. You know you have an enemy that you cannot see, but he is real. You have demons that are fighting against you and setting traps for you every day and in the future as well. He works through people to come against you. The only way you can defeat the devil is with God and his Word with the help of the Holy Spirit. You cannot fight the devil in the flesh; you must come after him in the Spirit. Gifted people realize when the devil comes against them, it is time for them to go into spiritual warfare using the Word of God, the Holy Spirit, Jesus and many prayer warriors and intercessors. You may be a single parent and have no one to help you raise your kids, but don't let that stop you from going to school and pursuing the dream that God has given you. So what if you had a child out of wedlock? God is still a forgiving God and you can still be successful in life and in your relationship with God. Don't let having a child outside of marriage cause you to not be who God has called you to be. You still have the victory in Christ Jesus. You may have been hurt so many times, but God can heal your heart and deliver you and set you free from all of your hurt and pain. You are too gifted to be depressed, you are too gifted to be on drugs, you are too gifted to be a homosexual or lesbian, you are too gifted to be a prostitute or an alcoholic, you are too gifted to walk in unforgiveness or bitterness, jealousy and hatred. You are just too gifted. Start telling yourself that right now. You are too gifted to be defeated.

CHAPTER TWENTY-TWO
YOU AIN'T FINISHED YET

– Daniel 3:1-28 –

In this passage of scripture, you find three amazing Jews with confidence in the God of Israel, who is the Almighty God, and the one and only true God. They were so confident in their God until nothing could shake them. They had a firm and solid foundation in the Lord. God is calling us to be like these three Hebrew boys and have a firm foundation in him until nothing can shake us. In this chapter, you will find faith, courage, patience, confidence and determination. The three Hebrew boys had faith in God; they had courage within themselves because of their God. They were confident in their God, they were patient in their God and lastly they were determined to show their God was a sustaining God and was a God that was on their side. Here you have a king by the name of

Nebuchadnezzar who made an image of gold ninety feet high and nine feet wide. The text says that he summoned the satraps, prefects, governors, advisers, treasurers, judges, magistrates and all the other provincial officials to come to the dedication of the image he had set up. (Daniel 3:1-3) The satraps were governors over major divisions of the empire serving as the chief representatives of the king. The prefects were the governors over conquered cities; they were civil administrators over provinces. The king expected everyone to bow down to this image he had made.

That is what the devil of today wants you to do; bow down to the 21st Century image he has made up for you today. You must not bow down to whatever it is that the enemy will seek to throw at you. You have bowed down to the devil long enough. Now it is time for you to fight him and go through your fiery furnace, like these three Hebrew boys did. If you do that, then you will come out with the victory. The devil has set up a golden image for you; it is called the image of destruction. He is trying to destroy you with the sins of the world because he wants your soul. The devil makes the sins of this world look so good to you. He makes it feel good and even makes it seem like it is right. He has so many other people doing it until he slowly lures you into sin. The devil causes you to do what everyone else is doing so you can try and fit in with the crowd, but really you are not being yourself. You are not being who God wants you to be; you are not being who God created you to be. I have noticed that people, even those in the body of Christ, are not being themselves and trying to be like other people. God is calling you to be like you. He didn't create you to be like no one else but yourself. In this world, you have so many people telling you that you should be this and you should be that. It has been going on for so many years. I am not saying that you shouldn't take people's advice; we need each other, but you should pray and ask God who you are supposed to be and what your purpose is on this earth. People can cause you to be something that God hasn't called you to be. That will get you into big trouble. One of the best ways a person can help you is for them to lead you to God and seek God for who you are supposed to be in this life.

You have to trust in the Lord with all of your heart. When you begin to trust in the Lord with all of your heart, that opens you up to his guidance. The way God guides you is by his Holy Spirit. You cannot lean to your own understanding. When you lean to your own understanding and go along with the intellect of man or receive advice from someone that does not give Godly counsel, you are setting yourself up for failure. In all your ways acknowledge him. In order for your life to change, you have to know that he is true and trust him with your life. God already knows what you are to be in the future.

God knows what ministry you are called to. God knows your destiny and purpose. You don't know what you are to be, but he knows what you are to be. If you trust him and stop trying to do things your way like king Nebuchadnezzar, then you will find out your destiny and purpose in life.

In this passage, you have a king that is confused. One minute he was accepting who God is and then the next minute he went right back to idol gods and doing things his way. The king made this image right after Daniel in interprets his dream and then he acknowledged Daniel's God. When things calmed down, he went right back to his old way of living. That is how a lot of people are today; things will get so bad in their lives and they will call on God. Then God will answer and bring them out. Then when things calm down and get back to normal, they go right back into the world. This is what king Nebuchadnezzar did; he wanted everyone who was connected to him to worship this golden image he had set up in Babylon. The Bible says that the herald, who is an announcer or a messenger, said, "At what time ye hear the sound of the cornet, flute, harp, sackbut, psaltery, dulcimer, and all kinds of music, ye fall down and worship the golden image that Nebuchadnezzar the king hath set up." (Daniel 3:5)

How many times in life have you allowed the devil to cause you to bow down and worship his images and his sinful lifestyle? You may have worshiped the image of money, the image of fornication (sex out of marriage), gambling, homosexuality; those are all images of the devil and God hates those types of images. I must tell you that even if you are a sinner, God still loves you. Does he want you to come out of the sin that is holding you in bondage? Yes, he does. He wants you out of those sinful acts because God loves you, but he hates sin. God literally hates sin. He loves the person that is in sin, which is why he died for you, so you could be saved from the sins and addictions and bad habits that have you bound by the devil. This book is to show you love, to reveal the truth, to expose sin, to rebuke, to warn you, to show you love, to encourage you, and to draw you to God. For the people who are already saved, but you may not be seeking God like you should, then this book is to draw you closer to Jesus Christ. Even believers can make their pastor their God by trusting the pastor more than they do God. That is not a good thing at all. Your pastor is there to teach you to trust in God and to trust God's Word. The pastor is a mouthpiece for God and God is over him. You need to realize that you need God more than anything. The pastor can't heal you if you get sick. All the money in the world can't heal you if you get sick; only Jesus can heal you.

It seems like God's people were consistently being tested, only to show the idol worshiping people that the God of Israel, the True and Almighty God, was the one and True God. The king's people came and denounced the Jews, who were Shadrach, Meshach, and Abednego. They said they would not worship the golden image. (Daniel 3) They appeared before the king because the king's officials said they worship and pay no any attention to his image. King Nebuchadnezzar became very angry and furious. They would not bow to his golden image and the king was furious. They said, "If it be so, our God whom we serve is able to deliver us from the burning fiery furnace, and he will deliver out of thine hand, O king. But if not, be it known unto thee, O king, that we will not serve thy gods, nor worship the golden image which thou hast set up." (Daniel 3:17-18) That is great faith. Shadrach, Meshach and Abednego's lives were on the line. They loved God so much and they were so committed to the God of Israel until they didn't bow down and worship his idol god. God is looking for some Shadrach, Meshach and Abednego people of today. God is calling his people to operate in the gift of faith. Faith will take you to deeper depths and higher heights in God. Sometimes God will put you in situations where your faith will be tested and it will strengthen your faith in God.

The three Hebrew men believed in their one and only True God. The truth of the matter is that they did not follow the crowd or try and fit in with everyone else; they sacrificed a bad way of living to live a righteous way of life. God is seeing if you want to sacrifice not following the crowd to live a holy and righteous life so you can go to heaven. I have discovered that even people in the church want to try and fit in with the crowd. That cannot be so. God is calling his people to be different. I am not saying you can't be in the world, but what I am saying is that God wants us to be an example for the world to see. God did not create you to fit in with everybody. He did create you to love everybody, to act like him and to be like him. If God loves, then we are to love. Since God forgave, then we are to forgive others who hurt us. If God can be loved, then we should be able to be loved. If God is just, then we should be just. If God tells the truth, then we should tell the truth. If God sacrifices, then we should sacrifice. If God is faithful, then we should be faithful. We should carry ourselves the way God carried himself in the Word of God. You learn more about God by getting into the Word of God, studying the Word of God for yourself, and seeking and asking questions from true and seasoned believers. You cannot expect to know God if you never spend any time with him. You can't expect God to reveal himself to you in his Word if you don't ever read his Word. You can't expect God to elevate you or cause you to know him better if you won't ever pray and seek his face. The same way you seek worldly things, you should reverse it and seek God the same way; then he will definitely reveal himself to you.

Here in this story, you find these three Hebrew boys executing faith. They said the God they serve is able to save them from this fiery furnace. That is what God is calling you to do; he is calling you to walk by faith and not by what you see. No matter what the situation looks like, make sure you exercise your faith in God. God will bring you out; just make sure you have faith in God. The situation isn't bigger and more powerful than God; there is nothing too hard for God. The situation you are in is going to get better; you just have to draw closer to God and God will come to your rescue. He will give you that peace in the midst of your storm and situation. God wants you to close your eyes and use the weapon of faith. When you use the weapon of faith, it will take you through anything you will ever encounter in this life. Faith gives you hope that one day things will get better, even when it seems like it won't.

Nowhere in this story does it indicate that these three Hebrew boys had a lack of faith. If they would have had a lack of faith, then they would have submitted to the image the king had set up. The revelation to this is that you can exercise your faith in God when your back is up against the wall. When you find yourself faced with your storm, just pull out your weapon of faith. That will bring you through any storm that you will ever face. These three Hebrew men's lives were on the line and they still did not worship this golden image that king Nebuchadnezzar had set up. That is so powerful and we can learn so much from them. Can you serve God even if you are about to spiritually go in the fiery furnace? When the devil is throwing a fiery furnace trial your way, will you still not bow to his image even though it seems like a defeat-like situation? It seemed like these three Hebrew boys were going to lose, but the hand of God was with them and they found favor with God. When you find favor with God, you can make it through every storm and every test that life has to offer you. The devil has many images in this world today which are causing people to bow down and fall into temptation, but there is a better way besides his way. I declare to you today that it may seem like things aren't going your way, but you are not finished yet. This thing is not unto death; you have a work to do. Get up out of your dilemma and be who God has called you to be. You were created to succeed in life; you were created to bless others; you are a blessing and not a curse. So what if your daddy wasn't there when you were little? You are still destined for greatness. You may have lost some things, you may have been hurt, you may be under attack, but it's still not over. You are not a loser, you are a winner.

The devil tried so hard to take these three Hebrew boys out, but God had a plan for their life and God still had work for them to do, even in an ungodly environment. They were in the Babylonian kingdom, but that kingdom wasn't in them. Just because you are in a bad environment doesn't mean you have to be like the environment you are in. You may be in the tightest situation right now and it may seem like you are walking in defeat, but if you just grab hold of God and have faith in him, then I promise your life will never be the same again. You have a work to do for the Lord. I don't care what it looks like; it's not over yet. You're not going anywhere because you have a work to do for the Lord. God created you to be a follower of Jesus. He created you to be a disciple. We are all disciples. As long as we are living, we will still be learning something concerning the Word of God. No one or no preacher has all the answers; only God has all the answers. If a pastor, preacher or minister acts like they have all the answers, you need to beware; that is a problem and a sign of pride and not humility. Being a very young pastor myself, I will be the first to tell you that I don't have all the answers. There are things in the Word of God that I don't comprehend or understand, but God knows everything. As a Pastor, I will always lead God's people to Jesus.

King Nebuchadnezzar thought it was over for these three Hebrew boys, but the Almighty God showed up and showed out for these young men. It was their faith that got them through the fire. For you, it is your faith in Jesus Christ that will take you through the fire in life. There may be a fire in your life right now. Your fire may be different things that this life has pushed on you. You may be having a fire of not being able to get over your past because it is so ugly, but by you having faith in God now, he will bring you through the fire. The king became furious. That is what the enemy will do when you start to activate your faith when being under attack by him. He gets upset, but there is nothing the devil can do when you operate in faith. When you operate in faith, believe in God, and start living for God, he is defeated. When you make it up in your mind that you are going to live for God that is when the devil will start to send things your way to try and keep you from living for God. Let's say you have had several addictions, but through faith and giving your life to Jesus you have been delivered. The devil will try to send the sins you used to do to bring you back into bondage. Please be careful because the devil is very sneaky. There is power when you press your way to Jesus. Just like when you would press your way to sin, you now need to press your way to Jesus Christ. Jesus is the only one who can deliver you and set you free. The only way to heaven is through Jesus Christ. You must believe in Jesus by faith. Even though you have never seen Jesus, you still have to have the faith to know that he exists and that he is sitting on the right hand of our Father who is in heaven.

One thing I noticed about these three Hebrew men who were placed in the fiery furnace is that they were confident in themselves that God would deliver them. It looked like they were in defeat, but the whole time they had the victory. Because they had faith in God, they came out with the victory. The reason why they were confident in themselves was because of their relationship with God. One thing I realize is that you can be confident in yourself when you have a relationship with God. Having a relationship with God causes you to be confident in who you are as an individual.

King Nebuchadnezzar ordered that the furnace be heated seven times hotter than usual and commanded some of the strongest soldiers to tie them up. They were tied up and bound physically, but they were not tied up and bound spiritually. Because they were not bound spiritually, they got free physically. (Daniel 3:19-20) The furnace was so hot that even the soldiers that took Shadrach, Meshach and Abednego up were killed by the furnace. The devil may have turned the furnace of your storm up seven times hotter, but you still will not be consumed by it. The God of Israel, Abraham, Isaac and Jacob will not let you be consumed by your fiery furnaces in life. You are not finished yet. You have been through a lot, but it's not over for you because God is on your side. As a very young pastor, I believe in you. I know you can do it. I know you can make it. I don't care what your past is, I still believe in you. I love you so much and I believe God for every reader who reads this book. When these three Hebrew boys were thrown into the fiery furnace the king said, "Did not we cast three men bound into the midst of the fire?... Lo, I see four men loose, walking in the midst of the fire, and they have no hurt; and the form of the fourth is like the Son of God." (Daniel 3:24-25) Nebuchadnezzar went up to the fiery furnace and told the three Hebrew men to come out. Everyone saw that the fire had not harmed them and it looked like they were never in the fire. Nebuchadnezzar praised the three Hebrew boys and their God.

The revelation to this is that you can go through so much in this life and you can be placed in the fiery furnace of your problem, but God can bring you out and it will look like your trial or storm never got to you. Praise be to God! Praise our Lord and Savior Jesus who will see you through anything!! Hallelujah!!! Thank You Jesus!! You are worthy!! Just start praising God right now and giving him the glory and watch him reveal himself to you and show himself to you in due time. You should make it up in your mind that you are going to be true to God no matter what the devil throws your way. If you are faithful to God no matter what the enemy will throw your way, then you will be rewarded by God. This fourth person they saw was obviously supernatural. Scholars aren't exactly sure who the fourth person was, but it could have been an angel sent from God. What you can get out of this situation is that when the devil attacks you, God will always send help to you. You are not defeated. You will make it. You will succeed in this life; just have faith because you are not finished yet.

CHAPTER TWENTY-THREE

DON'T LOOK BACK NOW

– Matthew 27:27-44 –

Here in this passage, you find the religious leaders condemning Jesus. We all know that Jesus was innocent and without sin. People may ask how we know that Jesus Christ was without sin when we weren't there when he was living. How can he be perfect when he was human? He was perfect because he was fully God as well. God doesn't have to show us or give us every little detail about him. Either you believe in the Word of God or you don't. The Bible says, "In the beginning was the Word, and the Word was with God, and the Word was God. The same was in the beginning with God." (John 1:1-2) When I say in the beginning was the Word and that he was with God in the beginning, I am referring to Jesus. Jesus is the Word. "The Word was made flesh, and dwelt among us." (John 1:14)

In other words, Jesus became a human and descended here to the earth. There is theology, which is the study of God, Christology, the study of Christ, and pneumatology, the study of the Holy Spirit. They all go together and you cannot separate them. God is who sent his son Jesus down on earth. His son Jesus sent and baptized people in the Holy Ghost. (John 15:26, John 14:16, John 16:7) We understand and comprehend that Jesus had to ascend so he could send the Holy Spirit. Without the Holy Spirit, you have no power to defeat satan and to live a victorious Christian life. Without Jesus, there is no salvation and man cannot be redeemed or saved from the pit of hell. Without God, there can be no Jesus because Jesus is the Son of God. You now see that they go together. This is where you get into the Trinity, which is the Father, Son, and Holy Spirit; you can't separate the three. The Trinity is the main source of the Christian faith; they cannot be separated from each other. I don't want to get in too deep about this subject because I don't want to do that in this book. If you don't believe in this concept of God, then it is impossible to exegete the Word of God correctly.

God sent his Son Jesus Christ on this earth to suffer and die for your sins so you would have a chance to go to heaven. Notice I said have a chance. I say that because there will not be many people that will go to heaven. (Luke 13:24-28) There are going to be a lot of people who are not going to make it into heaven. That is so dangerous. It isn't hard to go to heaven, but you have to sacrifice living a sinful life to start living a holy life. In the world we live in today, so many people gamble with their lives and think they are invincible. People are dying every day and many of them are not saved when they die. Many people get so caught up in the cares of this world until they neglect their spiritual life. There has to be a balance. If you really love God, you will make time for God. Anything that you love the most, you will make time for. If you love God, then you will make time for God. There are 24 hours in a day; you can at least take time out of your day and give God an hour if you really love him. If he really means that much to you, then you would give him the time he deserves.

In this passage, all the chief priests and elders of the people came to the decision to put Jesus to death. Jesus is at the climax of his ministry and his ministry on earth is over. They bound him, led him away and handed him over to Pilate, the governor. They may have bound him physically, because he was fully human as well, but they could not bind him spiritually, because Jesus is fully God as well. Jesus was sent by God his Father to die for this world. When Jesus came on the earth, he became limited to time and space, but his father was not limited to time and space. Being that his Father was not limited to time in space still made Jesus in control because he was fully God as well. So you had God in time and space, but not limited to time and space because he was connected to the Father. When Judas saw that they seized Jesus, he then went back and tried to reverse the problem and offered the thirty pieces of silver back to them, but they said it was his responsibility and not theirs. Judas could not forgive himself and he went and hung himself. If Judas Iscariot could have forgiven himself, I believe that maybe God could have used him mightily as well and that he could have been an effective Apostle in that time. Now notice I said maybe.

That is what the devil is seeking to do with you; he is trying to make you not forgive yourself for the sins you have done like Judas did and then he wants you to spiritually hang yourself. So many people commit suicide simply because they can't forgive themselves or other people. They feel like they have no hope, but that is only a trick of the enemy. Don't be a Judas. Judas was a betrayer because he betrayed Jesus and satan entered into Judas. You have come too far to turn back now. God has brought you out of so much trouble and now this is your chance to be who God has called you to be. It seems like the worst keeps happening, but don't look back now. Just press forward because your future is much brighter than your past.

Look back at the beginning of this book where I was telling you about my life; look at what God has done. If God can do it for me, then he can definitely do it for you. I was lost and I was on my way to hell. When I was lost, did I know I was on my way to hell? No, I didn't know, but thank God for the Holy Spirit convicting me of my sins. I knew I needed to change but I didn't know how. God started dealing with me. Today I am a young pastor, evangelist, author and a husband with a very anointed, sweet, precious and humble wife. God has placed an awesome Bishop over my church. His name is Bishop Vander D. Purcell and he has been in ministry over 50 years. He has poured into me so much. If it weren't for God and my Bishop, I wouldn't be where I am today. He has poured the Word of God into me. He and my wife believed in me when no one else would. When you make it up in your mind that you are going to live for God and don't look back, God will then send people like my wife and my Bishop into your life to help you on your journey. You may say, "None of my friends are saved." You may say, "None of my family members are saved." That still is no excuse. If you are serious about your relationship with God, then God will place people into your life that will help you grow in God. When I made it up in my mind that I was going to live for God, I called all my unsaved friends that I used to sin with. When I told them I got saved and that I was going to live for God and not do the things I used to do, all of them turned their backs on me.

When you make it up in your mind that you are going to live for God, you will see who your true friends are. Anyone that is your true friend and anyone who really loves you will tell you to get your life right with Jesus and get in a church where the true Word of God is being preached. That is one of the things that drew me to my Bishop; he preaches the Gospel of Jesus Christ. He always preaches Jesus; that is what made me sit under his ministry. Even now, he is over 30 plus churches and he still meets with us preachers for a whole hour before Bible study each week. He believes in developing aspiring preachers and pastors. These are the kinds of bishops and pastors we need; the ones who will pour into the upcoming ministers. You have come too far to turn back now. Don't give up and don't give in. Give no place to the devil. When you find yourself being faced with your addictions and flesh issues that is when you need to call on Jesus and try him. I dare you to try Jesus. If you try him, he will manifest himself in your life. You will be tested to see if you will stick with Jesus Christ. God allows you to be tested so you can see where you are. If you ever fail a couple of tests, then don't feel bad. Just dust yourself off and keep on trying. God wants you to see what is in your heart.

Jesus stands trial before Pilate, and the governor asked him, "Art thou the King of the Jews?" (Matthew 27:11) Jesus could have said no and not went through what he was about to endure, but Jesus says, "Thou sayest." (Matthew 27:11) Even in the most terrible situation, Jesus didn't look back. Instead, he looked at the big picture. He knew he was the Savior of mankind. In the most terrible situation, Jesus never once denied who he was. Can you stick with Jesus even in the most terrible situation? Peter denied Jesus three times and he failed the test, but God still used him mightily. Peter had to forgive himself before he could go forth in ministry. You cannot be effective in ministry if you are holding on to unforgiveness. If you are operating in jealousy towards someone and operating in pride, you cannot be effective in ministry. You also cannot be effective in your relationship with Jesus Christ. When you are in the fire of your situation, will you make a stand for Jesus? Some Christians get around other Christians and act saved, but when they get around people who are not Christians, then they act like the unsaved, just to gain approval from the world. If you have to gain approval from the worldly friends by doing what they do, then they really were not your friends in the beginning. We are living in a world where people don't want to stand and live by the truth and reality. The truth is that Jesus is real; the truth is that Jesus is the Son of the Living God; the truth is the only way to heaven is through Jesus; the truth is that there is a hell. This world is living on false hopes and being deceived by the devil.

Jesus said nothing to the chief priests and elders when they accused him; they falsely accused him anyway. They were determined to kill him. They so badly wanted to kill him, not just because they said he blasphemed, when he didn't, but they wanted to kill him because he was gifted and claimed to be the Son of the Living God. Once people find out you are gifted, you can't expect everyone to be happy for you. Jesus went around healing the sick, casting out demons and even the demons were subject to his name. Jesus gave sight to the blind, raised the dead and fed thousands. In him doing all of that, he became very popular and a lot of people wanted to follow him because of the great miracles he had done. The religious leaders and Pharisees got jealous because it took the focus off of them and on to an ordinary man who looked poor. These religious leaders claimed to be of God and claimed to be holy, but Jesus called them hypocrites. That is exactly what they were. If they were of God, then they would have been happy when Jesus was healing the sick, raising the dead and casting out devils. Instead, they wanted all the attention on them.

That is the problem with some people today; they scheme their way to the top rather than trusting God to make a way for them.

They had Jesus flogged and severely beaten and they insulted him tremendously. Can you imagine being insulted and beaten and spit on, knowing you have done nothing wrong? This is what our Savior Jesus went through for us. He got persecuted for being who God had called him to be. When you be yourself and be who God has called you to be, a lot of people won't like that, but you still have to be who God has called you to be. For the readers who are in the process of changing, I warn you: once you change, people aren't going to want to accept the new you, but you can't let that stop you from changing. You are on your way to heaven and you cannot let other people or family members cause you to miss out on heaven. We are living in a world where some people always want to compare you to other people. Don't let what you see the world doing distract you from being you and who God has called you to be. Nobody else can be you but you. Why not just be you? How bad do you want Jesus in your life? How bad do you want to get closer to him? Are you tired of living a complacent life? Do you want to go forth into what God has ordained for your life? God is calling you into total submission to him; the same way you submit to your boss is the same way God is calling you to submit to him. If you don't submit to your boss, you won't have a job. The wonderful thing about Jesus is that even if you don't submit to Christ, he still won't give up on you. He will love you no matter what you do and no matter how foolish you act. That is a loving God.

The soldiers started mocking Jesus and they sent Jesus into the governor's house and gathered the whole company of soldiers around him. There were about two hundred soldiers who were around him and they stripped him, put a scarlet robe on him and mocked him consistently. How many times have you let Jesus down, time after time and again? Yet he still keeps giving you chance after chance after chance, extending his love, grace and mercy towards you. Jesus says, "I will not leave you comfortless." (John 14:18) Jesus said he must go back to the Father so he can send the Holy Ghost and so his disciples and the believers to come will have power over demons. The Holy Ghost is who gives you power over the devil. It is the Holy Ghost that lets you know who is for you and who is not for you. Without the direction and leading of the Holy Ghost, you will get hurt and will be lost. The Holy Ghost leads you and guides you and protects you from the devil's schemes and traps. Everyone that comes into your life isn't necessarily supposed to be in your life. Some people just get weak and vulnerable and allow the wrong kind of people into their lives and then end up hurt.

Jesus came this far, all the way up to his crucifixion and he didn't look back at all. I am encouraging you to not look back. I am not telling you to forget where you came from, but don't let your past hinder you from where God is trying to take you. Don't look back now! Kiss your past goodbye! Your past is your past so let it be and let go and let God have his way in your life. You have made it this far in your life and it was God that caused you to make it to where you are now. Many of you should have been in some should-have-been-dead situations, but it is the power of God and his angels that have protected you. Thank God for protection and thank God for his angels. God is saying hold on to him, don't look back, it's over now; let the past be the past. Jesus said, "Follow me; and let the dead bury their dead." (Matthew 8:22) The revelation to that is to follow after Jesus; in following after Jesus, you must know and understand that he demands your total submission and obedience to him. I am not saying you give up everything that he has blessed you with, but what I am saying is you give up your sinful lifestyle that is separating you from God. You must know and understand that sin does separate you from God. I tell you in the name of Jesus Christ our Lord and Savior to pick up your cross, let go of the sinful acts of disobedience and deny yourself and don't look back anymore. This is your season, if you want it to be. How bad do you want Jesus Christ in your life? Do you trust in him and believe in him for him to have total control of your life?

CHAPTER TWENTY-FOUR

WHEN THE GOING GETS TOUGH

– Nehemiah 2:1-20 –

There are times in life where it seems like a lot of things just don't make sense at all. You don't always understand why certain things happen to you in this life. A lot of times, the going just gets so tough. Some of you may be believers and you wish you could just have a meeting with God and he tell you the next thing that is going to happen in your life. You wish God would tell you what is about to happen next, but yet you are left in suspense. It seems like things can be going good for a while for you and then all of a sudden an unwarned storm will pop up in your life, making you wonder if God is really there. I will be the first to admit that there were so many times, even while being a Christian that I wondered if God was really there. You can be having a good day and then you hear some bad news and it can mess up your whole day. When the going gets tough, you have to rely on Jesus Christ to bring you through the tough moments of your life. If you come down with cancer or lose a loved one, then you really have to rely on Jesus Christ to bring you healing. When my grandparents died, I thought I would never get over it, but God brought me out. Life has its way of getting the best of us at times, but you can't let what you are going through cause you to stay in defeat. There are brighter days ahead. I know it may not look like it all the time, but there are brighter days ahead for you. In the name of Jesus, it will get better for you. It may have already started to get better for you.

The trials and storms in life are only to make you stronger and to draw you closer to God. When you start thinking about what tests and trials you are in, just have a flash back on where God has brought you from. Know that if he did it then, he can do it again. God can pull you out of the dirtiest pit if you will allow him to. I am a witness to that; my life was in a pit, but the power of God brought me out. Now I am a very young pastor, evangelist and Christian author spreading the Gospel of Jesus Christ. Year after year has gone by and each year you thought it was your year, only to find out that there was something that came up and hindered you. You must understand and know that there will be storms in life and there will always be certain things that you will have to face; storms are a part of life. Whatever you believe God for, make sure it is according to his will for your life. If it is, then be patient and receive it from God by faith.

In this passage, you find Nehemiah in distress because he found out that the wall in Jerusalem was torn down. God's people, the Jews, were taken captive. There were some that escaped and they were deeply concerned about Jerusalem. Once Nehemiah heard what happened, he sat down and wept and mourned for days and he fasted and prayed. I encourage you that when you take the time to pray like Nehemiah did and seek the face of God, you can look for God to move on your behalf. Nehemiah sought the face of God and prayed so much. Because Nehemiah prayed and sought God with a pure heart and with pure motives, God gave him a plan and a vision. When you seek the face of God with a pure heart and with right motives, he will give you a plan and vision for your life. The plan and vision that God gave him was to go to Jerusalem and rebuild the wall. It took 52 days to build this wall. What seemed impossible to man became possible to man. This task was very difficult and the going was very tough, but Nehemiah didn't let how difficult this task seemed make him not proceed to do it. Just because something seems difficult to you, it doesn't mean you can't do it. You can do anything you put your mind to do. Nehemiah didn't let the toughness of this terrible situation hinder him from doing what God had called him to do.

You as a believer must not let what you see in this world and what happens in your life cause you to forfeit your destiny and purpose in your life. Nehemiah was a man of God and he served the king. He had a good relationship with the king and that helped him be released to do his work. This wall in Jerusalem was destroyed. Perhaps your wall has been torn down in your Jerusalem, from a spiritual perspective. Maybe your wall of faith has been torn down and now God is wonting to send you a Nehemiah to rebuild your wall in your life. God wants to build you a wall of blessings. You need a Nehemiah in your life to help you rebuild your wall. The word Nehemiah means Jehovah comforts. The Lord has come to comfort you, no matter what you are going through. Wine was before him and Nehemiah took the wine and gave it to the king. Nehemiah was sad in the king's presence. Nehemiah found out what happened to Jerusalem and he wept for days. You may have had a lot of weeping moments in your life where you have cried and cried and cried, but God wants to rebuild your wall. The devil has beat on you long enough; enough is enough. After you weep and cry and mourn, it is time for you to dry up your tears and get down on your knees and fight the devil in the spirit. Nehemiah wept, mourned and cried, but after all of that he did something about it. He got permission from the king to go and rebuild the wall in Jerusalem.

It's time for you to rebuild your wall. It doesn't matter what wall has been torn down in your life, God can still rebuild it if you will allow him to. Perhaps you are not saved and you want to get saved; you want God to start rebuilding your wall spiritually. I am referring to getting your life in order, getting you in the will of God, getting you into obedience. The king said to Nehemiah, "Why is thy countenance sad, seeing thou art not sick? This is nothing else but sorrow of heart." (Nehemiah 2:2) In other words, the king knew something was bothering Nehemiah and he knew he wasn't sick. That is why you can't let the devil get the best of you when he is attacking you. When you are under attack by the devil that is when you need to put him in the chokehold and choke him with the Word of God. Don't let the devil see you sweat. When you are under attack that is when you need to call on the name of Jesus. Even if you don't know how to pray when you are going through, just call on the name of Jesus. Find a mature Christian and a true church where you can become a disciple. Nehemiah tells him what happened and then the king asks him what his request was.

When you develop a relationship with God, you can request anything from him that is in the will of God. It must be in his will and be in line with the Word of God. Nehemiah tells him about wanting to go to Judah to complete this task. The king then asks Nehemiah how long it will take to do it and when he will return. He set him a time, but because of the favor of God, Nehemiah was released to go. No matter what atmosphere you are in, when the favor of God is upon your life, you must walk in abundance. Nehemiah was appointed governor of Judea by the Persian emperor and soon afterward he came to Jerusalem. In addition, he was given a military escort and government funding by Artaxerxes to aid in the building of the wall around Jerusalem. What you can learn from this book is that the Lord can sometimes use people who are not in his will to do a work for his people. All you have to do is go to Jesus for him to rebuild your wall. God will do it; you have the tool of faith and you also have the tool of hope. Nehemiah goes to Jerusalem in faith and not discouragement. He deals with this issue like he already has the victory. He had the victory for the God that he served. That is how you have to be; you have to go up against your situations and problems like you already have the victory. The truth is that you do have the victory. He has one thing in mind that he won't let anything stop him from achieving his difficult task. These people were the children of Israel and it seemed like all hope was gone for them, but God used one man to restore. When he went out for his journey he didn't have any help, but God gave him the vision to rebuild and God also sent the people he needed to fulfill the vision he gave Nehemiah.

What I have realized is that God will give you the vision and won't tell anyone else but you. Then he will send people into your life to help you to fulfill the vision that he wants to fulfill through you. If you hold on and keep the faith you will reap the harvest of blessing if you faint not. Just don't give up. When the going gets tough, please don't give up. When it gets more difficult, then that is the time to really come closer to Jesus. When they were rebuilding the wall, they had a sword in one hand and were working with the other hand. Their enemies were Sanballat and Tobiah. Sanballat was an opponent of Nehemiah; he was an enemy. He was a satrap of Samaria. Tobiah was a servant. These were two men that didn't want to see this wall rebuilt. What you must learn from this is that there are and will always be people that will not want you to fulfill the vision that God has given you. That is why you can't be so quick to tell people what God has called you to do because everybody won't be happy for you. There will always be a Sanballat and a Tobiah in your way that are trying to keep you from rebuilding your wall in your life. No matter what, when the going gets tough, just start rebuilding your life with Jesus Christ. Rely on him to change your life and draw you closer to him.

CHAPTER TWENTY-FIVE

RECEIVING WISDOM

– Proverbs 2:1-14 –

True wisdom comes from God. The only way you can receive true wisdom is from God. It is through God, the Son and the Holy Spirit that you obtain Godly wisdom. You cannot have Godly wisdom without God; you cannot have Godly wisdom without Jesus or without the Holy Spirit. They all intricately go together. The purpose of proverbs is to reveal wisdom to the people of God and to show them that without God, you are nothing. It is God who defines who you are; it is God who judges you and only he alone can judge you. The author of Proverbs is Solomon. He compiled most of these writings in his early reign as king and he rebuilt the temple. The book of proverbs will help you and aid you into making sound and Godly decisions. You may have knowledge, and knowledge is good, but knowledge without wisdom is useless. True wisdom comes from God. Solomon was the wisest man. He left us a legacy of written wisdom in three components called Proverbs, Ecclesiastes, and Song of Songs. You can have knowledge about God, but when you have wisdom from God's Word, then wisdom will call you to take the Word of God and apply it to your life. That is true wisdom.

True wisdom says when your boss is treating you mean, you will still show love and treat your boss with love and care. True wisdom will cause you to always do the will of God and be obedient and pleasing to God. Turn your ear to wisdom and apply your heart to understanding. When you turn your ear to Godly wisdom, then it makes you a better person and causes you to receive understanding. The people who accept Jesus Christ as their personal Lord and Savior begin to walk in true wisdom. You cannot have Godly wisdom if you don't have Jesus Christ first in your life. It doesn't matter if you go to church every Sunday; there are people who go to church every Sunday, but they still have no Godly wisdom. True wisdom comes in when you realize you need to have Jesus in your life and you get to a point in life that you are ready to surrender your life to Jesus Christ. True wisdom is something that doesn't come overnight; you can't expect wisdom to just jump in your lap when you ask for it. True wisdom is something that comes from God; you must prove to

God that you want Godly wisdom. If you say you want to be wise in God, but never pray, never read God's Word, never attend Bible study or never get active in ministry, then you are not showing God that you want Godly wisdom. You have to be willing to search for wisdom. The way you search for true wisdom is by seeking after God. When you seek after God, you are showing God that you want Godly wisdom.

Wisdom begins with God. God is the all wise God with all the wisdom in his very being. Fleshly people can never obtain true wisdom. True wisdom is from and starts with the Word of God. Just because you have knowledge about other religions doesn't mean you have true wisdom. True wisdom comes when you believe in Jesus Christ and take the Word of God and apply it to our life. God gives wisdom to people who seek after it; when you seek the face of God, he then starts to pour out his wisdom to you and he starts to reveal himself to you. People who are rebellious and sinful can never obtain wisdom from God. Disobedient and foolish people don't understand true wisdom and they can never receive it. It is in your maturing in God that you receive the wisdom of God. The more you mature in God, the more God will reveal himself to you. You will look up and you will be full of Godly wisdom. God wants to give wisdom to people who seek after him. God knows that it takes his wisdom to keep you and sustain you in this Christian walk. If you want to receive wisdom, make sure you show God that you are ready to receive his wisdom.

One of the things I have discovered is that you can go to seminary to learn the Word of God; you can go to Bible college and learn to become an eloquent speaker, but one thing you cannot go to school for is the power of God and the anointing of God. You cannot go to school for the power of God. In order to get the power of God, you must demonstrate humility and a life of prayer. God won't just give the power of God to anybody. I have discovered that there are so many people in the pulpit that have no power. It seems like they have power because of how many people like them, but Apostle Paul and the other Apostles were not liked by many people because they had a true relationship with God. One of the things you must realize is that when you make a stand for the Gospel of Jesus Christ, not everyone will like you for that. Many people today would rather live off of deception. There are so many people who live off of deception in this world. Deception means trickery or fraud. Fraud means to cheat. The devil is cheating people every day. He makes what isn't right look right. People go on this false hope that the sin that they are in is okay. In God's eyes it isn't okay. James says that whosoever is a friend of the world is the enemy of God. It is impossible to love the world and God too. You cannot serve two masters and you cannot love both the world and God at the same time. True wisdom says you will sacrifice your love for the world for Jesus Christ. Jesus Christ is the only one that can give you true wisdom and knowledge and understanding of the things of God. Jesus Christ can help you to make wise and Godly decisions based on the Word of God and prayer.

FINAL WORD

I hope and pray that you have received from this book. I put much thought and prayer into writing this book. My goal wasn't to judge or put anyone down, but it was to make you see the truth. It is the truth that will and can make you free. If you are not saved and you have read this book, you can now give your life to Jesus Christ and your life will never be the same. This book wasn't meant to be deep and theologically deep; it was meant to be simple so you can see the truth and see how much God really loves you; so you can see how much I really love you and how much I believe in you. I know you can make it. If you want to get saved, then you can get saved right where you are. Then find a church that is preaching the true Word of God and your life will never be the same. Then surround yourself with strong Christian believers. One thing you don't want to do is get saved and then the next day or week or month be right back into the world doing the same old sins you used to do. When you get saved, make sure you stay rooted and grounded. Don't just get saved right now and then don't find a church or don't ever read the Word of God. You have to be willing to make a commitment to God. The same way you committed to serving the devil, you now have to make that same commitment to serving God.

Repeat this simple prayer: Lord Jesus, I am a sinner. I confess all of my sins to you Lord Jesus. Lord Jesus, save me, deliver me, set me free. Lord Jesus, I confess with my mouth that you are the Son of the Living God. I believe in my heart that God raised you from the dead. By that power, I am saved. Lord Jesus, fill me with your Holy Spirit and keep me from going back into the world. Lord Jesus, keep me in your perfect will. I confess with my mouth and I believe in my heart that you are Jesus Christ, the Son of the Living God. Save me O Lord. Save me from the pit of hell. If you have prayed that simple prayer, then you are now saved. "That if thou shalt confess with thy mouth the Lord Jesus, and shalt believe in thine heart that God hath raised him from the dead, thou shalt be saved. For with the heart man believeth unto righteousness; and with the confession is made unto salvation." (Romans 10:9-10) You must believe in your heart that Jesus Christ is Lord. You must believe that he is the Son of the Living God. For those of you that may have fallen away, you can rededicate your life back to the Lord. Just think about the day and time when you first got saved; how on fire you were for the Lord. Let the Lord rekindle that fire. I want all of you to know that I love you so much and I believe in you. If no one else believes in you, I do. I know that there is a God and I know that Jesus is real. I hope and pray that this book has been a blessing to you. I encourage everyone to go out and receive this life changing message in this book. I am praying for you and I believe God for you. No matter what your past is, God can deliver you out of your past and still make you successful. I have been hurt by so many people. So many people didn't think I would make it. Look at what the Lord has done. When man says no, God says yes. You are created and ordained for success. You can make it and you will make it. May God bless you and I love you so much.

Printed in the United States
201890BV00003B/118-159/P